~~him, with hands stretch'd out upon the cross;~~
Divine compassion in his bosom glows.
He hears revilers with oblique regard
What Condescention in the Son of God!
When the whole human race, by Sin had fal'n;
He deign'd to Die, that they might rise again,
To live with him beyond the Starry Sky
Life without death, and Glory without End.—

Improve your privileges while they stay:
Caress, redeem each moment, which with haste
Bears on its rapid wing Eternal bliss.
Let hateful vice so baneful to the Soul,
Be still avoided with becoming care;
Suppress the sable monster in its growth,
Ye blooming plants of human race, divine
An Ethiop tells you, tis your greatest foe

The Poems of
PHILLIS WHEATLEY

✤✤✤✤✤✤✤

PHILLIS WHEATLEY, NEGRO SERVANT to Mr. JOHN WHEATLEY, of BOSTON.

The Poems of
PHILLIS WHEATLEY

✣✣✣✣✣✣✣✣✣✣✣✣✣✣✣✣✣✣✣

Edited with an Introduction by

JULIAN D. MASON, JR.

✣✣✣✣✣✣✣✣✣✣✣✣✣✣✣✣✣✣✣

THE UNIVERSITY OF
NORTH CAROLINA PRESS · CHAPEL HILL 1966

Library of Congress Catalog Card Number 66-15510

Manufactured in the United States of America

✤ CONTENTS ✤

PART TWO: MISCELLANEOUS POEMS

• ILLUSTRATIONS •

All illustrations are from the 1773 edition of *Poems on Various Subjects, Religious and Moral* in the Louis Round Wilson Library of the University of North Carolina at Chapel Hill.

INTRODUCTION

The primary purpose of this volume is to make readily available once more Phillis Wheatley's poems, which have become difficult to obtain even though most of them have been reprinted numerous times in limited editions. These poems were written by a young Negro slave in Boston in the last third of the eighteenth century and were generally well received at a time when even white women were not expected to be able to write such poems. Furthermore, she has been too often overlooked, particularly by our contemporary literary historians and anthologizers of American literature. While not exceptional in quality, these poems are almost as good as any that were published by Americans at that time, even though they are the work of one who had been brought from Africa as a child and had been speaking English only about ten years when she wrote most of her poems. That all of these facts pertain to the poems of Phillis Wheatley makes the accomplishing of the purpose of this volume almost mandatory in the face of a growing interest in the place of the Negro in American culture.

Phillis Wheatley was brought from Africa to Boston as a slave in 1761, when she was probably about seven years old, and was soon bought by John Wheatley, a respected tailor of Boston.[1] We do not know what her native land

1. Unless otherwise cited, the facts in this brief biographical sketch are cited in and sometimes are supplemented by one or more of the following sources: B. B. Thatcher, *Memoir of Phillis Wheatley, A Native African and a Slave* (Boston, 1834); [Margaretta Matilda Odell], *Memoir and Poems of Phillis Wheatley, A Native African and a Slave* (Boston, 1834, 1835, 1838); G. Herbert Renfro, *Life and Works of Phillis Wheatley* (Washington, 1916); Vernon Loggins, *The Negro Author* (New

was,[2] and she seems to have remembered little of her life before her arrival in this country—or at least to have refrained from mentioning any such memories—except for the interesting habit which her mother had of pouring out water as a libation to the rising sun.

Wheatley had several slaves, but he desired a young girl to be trained to attend his wife, Susannah. When Phillis was purchased, she was apparently rather frail and was dressed in scant clothing, and these conditions tended to make her a pitiful sight. However, under the supervision of Wheatley's daughter, Mary, Phillis soon began to emerge as a child worthy of attention and instruction. Indeed, her quickness of mind not only found favor in the eyes of the Wheatleys, but it also marked her for unusual notoriety among a gradually increasing segment of the Boston population. One of her biographers has declared:

> . . . it is probable that but few of the white children of Boston were brought up under circumstances better calculated for the full development of their natural abilities. Her ambition was stimulated: she became acquainted with grammar, history, ancient and modern geography, and astronomy, and studied Latin so as to read Horace with such ease and enjoyment that her French biographer [Grégoire] supposes the great Roman had considerable influence upon her literary tastes and the choice of her subjects of composition. A general interest was felt in the . . . prodigy; the best libraries were open to her: and she had opportunities for conversation with the most accomplished and distinguished persons in the city.[3]

York, 1931); and Benjamin Brawley, *The Negro in Literature and Art in the United States* (New York, 1934). Sketches of her life can also be found in many standard biographical dictionaries, including the *Dictionary of American Biography,* and in other volumes dealing with Negro writers and their works.

2. Although there has been some reference to her as a native of the Senegal region, this apparently cannot be substantiated.

3. Rufus Wilmont Griswold, *The Female Poets of America* (New York, 1877), p. 30.

Apparently, fortune had repented of having put Phillis into slavery and had placed her at the most propitious age in an environment appropriate for the cultivation of her native talents. Brawley says, "Mrs. Wheatley was a woman of unusual refinement. Her home was well known to the people of fashion and culture in Boston . . . ."[4] In a vein certainly more cautious and probably more accurate than that of Griswold, Brawley adds:

> Within sixteen months from the time of her arrival in Boston Phillis was able to read fluently the most difficult parts of the Bible. From the first her mistress strove to cultivate in every possible way her naturally pious disposition, and diligently gave her instruction in the Scriptures and in morals. In course of time, thanks especially to the teaching of Mary Wheatley, the learning of the young student came to consist of a little astronomy, some ancient and modern geography, a little ancient history, a fair knowledge of the Bible, and a thoroughly appreciative acquaintance with the most important Latin classics, especially the works of Virgil and Ovid. She was proud of the fact that Terence was at least of African birth. She became proficient in grammar, developing a conception of style from practice rather than from theory. Pope's translation of Homer was her favorite English classic. If in the light of twentieth century opportunity and methods these attainments seem in no wise remarkable, one must remember the disadvantages under which not only Phillis Wheatley, but all the women of her time, labored; and recall that in any case her attainment would have marked her as one of the most highly educated young women in Boston.[5]

It is generally supposed that Phillis was about thirteen years old when she began to try her hand at poetry. She was very much influenced by the poetry of the popular Alexander Pope, and her earliest attempt which has survived

4. *The Negro in Literature and Art,* p. 16.
5. *Ibid.,* pp. 17-18.

may be "On Being Brought from Africa to America." It is not strange that this slave girl should have been able to cultivate such an interest, for she came to be treated almost as a member of the family and was assigned only very light housekeeping tasks, with permission and encouragement to ignore even these duties when she felt poetically inclined. It is to her credit that such preferential treatment did not make her haughty, but rather fostered in her a strong attachment, respect, and concern for the members of the Wheatley family. It should also be noted that her fortunate circumstances apparently did not alienate the respect of her fellow slaves, despite the fact that she was accepted as a guest in the homes of some of the Wheatleys' friends and was allowed the unusual privilege of having both heat and light in her own room in the Wheatley home in deference to her relatively frail health and a memory apparently so untrustworthy as to make it desirable for her to commit her thoughts to paper as quickly as possible.

The year 1771 saw two very important events in the Wheatley household. Mary became the wife of the Reverend John Lathrop, and Phillis became a baptized communicant in the Old South Meeting House in Boston, a notable exception to the usual practice in this church of not allowing such a status to slaves. However, Phillis' health began to fail noticeably; and on the recommendation of the family physician for sea air, it was decided that she would join Mary's twin, Nathaniel, in a voyage to England which he had planned for May of 1773.

In 1770, Phillis had gained some notice through her first published poem, on the death of the famous preacher, George Whitefield, which she had addressed to the Countess of Huntingdon; and in 1773 it was the Countess who aided Phillis in meeting many notable members of English society of the day. It is significant that in this company her ability as an exceptional conversationalist gained her both favor and presents, among which were a copy of the 1770 Glasgow folio edition of *Paradise Lost,* given to her by the Lord Mayor of London, and a copy of Smollett's 1770 translation of *Don Quixote,* given to her by the Earl of Dartmouth, another of the prominent persons whom she met in London.[6] She was urged to stay in England for presentation at the court of George III, but when she learned that Mrs. Wheatley was ill and that she had been asked for, Phillis hastened back to America. However, before she departed, arrangements were apparently well under way for the publication of a volume of her poems, which appeared in London before the year 1773 ended.

In October, Phillis was back in Boston, her health not really much improved. In March of 1774, Mrs. Wheatley died. After this sad event, Phillis apparently did not consistently remain in the Wheatley household, and she definitely left the Wheatley house after Mr. Wheatley's death in March of 1778. In retrospect, we can see her return to America from England as a downward turning point in her life. This downward trend was alleviated to some degree by the publication and the reception of her book, by her very courteous reception in 1776 in Cambridge during a visit with General George Washington (a visit which had come as the result of his personal invitation in response to a complimentary poem she had sent to him), and by her marriage in April of 1778 to John Peters. However, the pleasure of this last event was too soon marred.

John Peters was an enigmatic Negro who seems to have tried his hand as a baker, a grocer, a doctor, and a lawyer, without having much training for them or much success with them. He is reported to have had somewhat grandiose notions and to have possessed a wig, a cane, and a feeling of being superior to labor. When Boston fell to the British,

6. *Dictionary Catalog of the Schomburg Collection of Negro Literature and History* (Boston, 1962), IX, 8251.

Phillis and her husband fled to Wilmington, Massachusetts, remaining there until it was safe to return to Boston. Because of the attitudes of her husband, she and her three children suffered from both poverty and social estrangement. Before the winter of 1783-84, the two older children had died; and during one part of 1784, Peters was in jail. Phillis turned to working in a cheap lodginghouse to earn food for herself and the last remaining child. On December 5, 1784, Phillis Wheatley Peters died in Boston, and her last child followed her in death in time to be buried with her in a grave whose location has since been lost to the world.

Apparently few, if any, of her old acquaintances were immediately aware of her death. However, it did not go unnoticed very long, for the *Independent Chronicle* on the next Thursday reported:

> Last Lord's Day, died Mrs. Phillis Peters (formerly Phillis Wheatley), aged thirty-one, known to the world by her celebrated miscellaneous poems. Her funeral is to be this afternoon, at four o'clock, from the house lately improved by Mr. Todd, nearly opposite Dr. Bulfinch's at West Boston, where her friends and acquaintances are desired to attend. [Mr. and Mrs. Wheatley and their children were all dead by this date.][7]

The Boston Magazine for December, 1784, noted her death in its obituary lists on page 630 as follows: "Mrs. Phillis Peters (formerly Phillis Wheatly [*sic*])." In the same issue, in the "Poetical Essays" section on pages 619 and 620, there appeared the following poem, which is reprinted in its entirety here only because it has heretofore been overlooked by her biographers:

7. Brawley, *The Negro in Literature and Art,* p. 31.

ELEGY ON THE DEATH OF A LATE CELEBRATED POETESS.

If conscious sense of genius yet remains,
Of lofty verse, and soft poetic strains;
Shall not the muse a grateful tribute rear.
And drop the silent, sympathetic tear?
If aught that glows within the friendly breast,
That weeps at tales of woe, or hearts opprest;
With me your sympathizing tribute pay,
And to her peaceful manes inscribe the lay.
Ye! who her talents and her virtues knew,
With grief's spontaneous tears her urn bedew.
She too comply'd with nature's sacred tye,
She gently wip'd the sorrow-streaming eye,
As if by heaven inspir'd, did she relate,
The souls grand entrance at the sacred gate!
And shall the honour, which she oft apply'd,
To other's reliques, be to hers deny'd?
O that the muse, dear spirit! own'd thy art,
To soften grief and captivate the heart,
Then should these lines in numbers soft array'd,
Preserve thy mem'ry from oblivion's shade;
But O! how vain the wish that friendship pays,
Since her own volumes are her greatest praise.
As Orpheus play'd the list'ning herds among,
They own'd the magic of his powerful song;
Mankind no more their savage nature kept,
And foes to music, wonder'd how they wept.
So PHILLIS tun'd her sweet mellifluous lyre;
(Harmonious numbers bid the soul aspire)
While AFRIC'S untaught race with transport heard,
They lov'd the poet, and the muse rever'd.
What tho' her outward form did ne'er disclose
The lilly's white, or blushes of the rose;
Shall sensibility regard the skin,
If all be calm, serene, and pure within?
But ah! can beauty, or can genius save?
Genius and beauty moulder in the grave.
The modest graces, and the richest bloom,
The solemn toll soon ushers to the tomb.
Such the sad ruins of the human race,

That reptiles riot on the fairest face!
Hither let pride its sure criterion view;
In vain shall virtue plead, or honour sue;
Hither let luxury and av'rice find,
A cure for the distemper'd canker'd mind.
  Tho' now the business of her life is o'er,
Tho' now she breaths and tunes her lyre no more;
Tho' now the body mixes with the clay;
The soul wings upward to immortal day;
Free'd from a world of wo, and scene of cares,
A lyre of gold she tunes, a crown of glory wears.
  Seated with angels in that blissful place,
Where she now joins in her Creator's praise,
Where harmony with louder notes is swell'd,
Where her soft numbers only are excell'd.

HORATIO

State Street, Dec. 1784.

Of special interest is the poet's focus on Phillis as an accepted Boston poetess and not merely as a freak that resulted from a slave's having encountered fortuitous circumstances.

When Phillis Wheatley's first published poem appeared in 1770, as far as we know only two other American Negroes had published anything. Both publications had come in 1760, one a fourteen-page pamphlet by Briton Hammon (which was destined to be his only publication), and the other an eighty-eight-line broadside poem by Jupiter Hammon, whose next publication would come in 1778 in praise of Phillis.[8] Therefore, it can be said with confidence that she was the first American Negro writer of any significance and that her book of poems in 1773 was probably the first book—and was certainly the first book of poetry—published by an American Negro author.

8. For further information about these, consult Loggins, *The Negro Author*. There is some possibility that James Albert Ukawsaw Gronniosaw may have published his narrative in 1770, although this date is not definite. See Dorothy Porter, "Early American Negro Writings: A Bibliographical Study," *PBSA,* XXXIX (3rd Quarter 1945), 198.

The 1770 poem was *An Elegiac Poem, on the Death of that celebrated Divine, and eminent Servant of Jesus Christ, the late Reverend, and pious George Whitefield, Chaplain to the Right Honourable the Countess of Huntingdon,* first published as a broadside in Boston.[9] Primarily because of its timeliness and the popularity of Whitefield, but also because of its quality, the poem was republished several times.

Her next published works were three broadside elegiac poems which help to illustrate the contention that she apparently became a kind of poet laureate to whom many of the domestic circles of Boston turned for occasional verse. *To Mrs. Leonard, on the Death of her Husband* appeared in 1771; *To the Rev. Mr. Pitkin, on the Death of his Lady,* in 1772; and *To the Hon'ble Thomas Hubbard, Esq.; On the Death of Mrs. Thankfull Leonard,* in January of 1773. During this period, her first magazine publication was also accomplished with a shorter version of the poem which was to appear in the 1773 volume as "On Recollection." This early version, called simply "Recollection," was published in *The London Magazine* for March, 1772 (XLI, 134-35). It is quite likely that its appearance either inspired or greatly encouraged the idea of publishing a volume of her poems, for the 1773 volume contains a letter from Wheatley to the publisher dated November 14, 1772.

There is no doubt that the volume of thirty-nine poems brought out in London in 1773 as *Poems on Various Subjects, Religious and Moral* was her most significant publication. Here are the core, the majority, and the best of the poems of Phillis Wheatley; and the little volume has enjoyed generally favorable reception and has been reprinted numerous times.

9. The bibliographical data given in this section, unless otherwise cited, can be verified and complemented in Porter, "Early American Negro Writings," 193-268; Dorothy Porter, *North American Negro Poets: A Bibliographical Checklist of Their Writings 1760-1944* (Hattiesburg, Mississippi, 1945); Loggins, *The Negro Author*; or in the periodicals cited.

Also in 1773 was published in Boston the broadside poem, *An Elegy, to Miss Mary Moorhead, on the Death of her Father, The Rev. Mr. John Moorhead.* In December, 1774, *The Royal American Magazine* of Boston published in its "Poetical Essays" section a poem by her addressed "to a gentleman of the navy," which was followed by his reply—to which she then gave a poetic reply in the January, 1775, issue of the magazine. In April, 1776, while Thomas Paine was its editor, *The Pennsylvania Magazine* of Philadelphia included her brief letter to General Washington and the poem of praise which she had written to him.

The September, 1784, *Boston Magazine* published her poem "To Mr. and Mrs.......................... on the Death of Their Infant Son," and two others appeared as small pamphlets in Boston in 1784: *An Elegy, Sacred to the Memory of That Great Divine, The Reverend and Learned Dr. Samuel Cooper* and *Liberty and Peace.* Dorothy Porter cites one other broadside poem as possibly written by her: *An Ode, On the Birth Day of Pompey Stockbridge* [n.p., n.d.].

It appears that another volume of poems by Phillis might have been published if her life had not been cut so short. (See the proposal which is reprinted in this volume [p. 111].) Since her death, one more of her poems has found its way into print: "On the Capture of General Lee," published in the *Proceedings of the Massachusetts Historical Society* for October, 1863.

A number of her letters have been published since her death, all of which are reprinted in the appendix to this volume. It is interesting to note from the list of letters in the proposal for a second volume of her poems that all but one of the extant letters are ones which she had not planned to publish with her poems. However, they are the only ones now available.

It is quite clear that Phillis Wheatley was not a great poet. She was not a poet in the classical Greek sense of maker, seer, creator, nor were her concerns really with Emerson's meter making argument or Poe's rhythmical creation of beauty. Phillis had aspirations, but she also knew her shortcomings; and her concerns were less august, less pretentious. Her primary endeavor was to put into rhythmical, poetic forms those thoughts which came to her or which were brought to her attention by the small crises and significant experiences of the people of Boston as they met life and death from day to day. Most of what she wrote of was not noted by the world outside of that city, though she occasionally did treat more general topics and there is some evidence that during and after the Revolution her poetic horizons may have been broadening.

On the basis of the poems which have survived her short career, she must be labeled as primarily an occasional poet, one interested in the clever crafting of verse. Such a craftsman is not as concerned with selecting topics and creating patterns as with taking a given or obvious topic and fitting it skillfully to an already existing pattern. However, if he is a good craftsman, he is distinctive in his own right and possesses a gift which is worthy of the world's attention, if not its lasting praise. Such was Phillis Wheatley's gift and her concern, and she was a better craftsman of verse than most of the others attempting the same type of thing in America in the 1770's, a time and place which certainly produced more craftsmen than true poets. Her reward was in immediate praise—not the type which echoes through the ages, but which appropriately sounds again from time to time for only brief periods.

Yet, some of her poems reveal an exceptional being producing exceptional poetry. Most of her best work is in her nonoccasional poems, certainly in her more philosophic ones. In this regard it is interesting to note that various commentators have chosen different ones of her small body of poems to praise as the best,[10] and almost all writers on this subject favor to some degree "An Hymn to the Morning" and "An Hymn to the Evening." One would also be amiss not to place in this company "On Virtue" and "Goliath of Gath," and each reader might wish to include yet others; for in certain complete poems and in parts of other poems, Phillis was able to surpass to a great degree what was at once both her great asset and her great liability—a favor for and a remarkable spontaneous ability to re-create the neoclassical poetic mode of Alexander Pope and his followers, in diction, meter, rhyme, and syntax. In such happy instances she avoided ordinary subject matter and cliches, using instead striking, appropriate poetic figures in pleasing form which attracted both the mind and the ear. In these she was more than just an imitator, and she reflected a fortunate influence of the best neoclassicism. Unfortunately, she could not write this well consistently enough for such good poetry to dominate her work, leaving her to be known primarily as a prodigious imitator. For the same poet who wrote the exceptional poems mentioned above also wrote too many run-of-the-mill elegies which, except for their historical interest, might now just as well be lost.

Phillis seems to have been fascinated with the device of invocation, and her mixing of Christian and classical in the many invocations in her poems (as well as in other parts of the poems too) reflects the two greatest influences on her work, religion and neoclassicism. Indeed, this device and a few others remind one of Milton, though she certainly does not use them with his skill. For example, one can see the mixing of the Christian and the neoclassic in "To Maecenas" and "On Recollection," and she apparently attempts the

10. For example: Loggins, p. 373, *n.* 75, calls "A Farewell to America" "perhaps her most graceful achievement in versification"; Brawley, *The Negro in Literature and Art,* p. 35, calls "On Imagination" her best poem; J. Saunders Redding, *To Make A Poet Black* (Chapel Hill, 1939), p. 12, favors "Thoughts on the Works of Providence."

Miltonic device of vague exactness in measurement in "Thoughts on the Works of Providence" when she says of the sun's distance from the earth, "Of miles twice forty millions is his height." Loggins has pointed to the influence of English writers on her poems dealing with imagination, recollection, and virtue and to the influence of Milton on her hymns to the morning and evening[11] and her poem about General Lee.[12] He also suggests the specific influence of Gray on her poem on Whitefield's death and of Addison and Watts on "Ode to Neptune" and "Hymn to Humanity."[13]

However, the strongest influences on her work definitely were that of religion (including the Bible) and that of neoclassicism. Phillis has been called a typical New Englander of the eighteenth century in her pious religious views, which seem to crop up everywhere. She is constantly aware of God, His Son, His beneficence, and His power; and she intends that her readers be aware of them too. Almost every poem produces a moral at some point, and the mood and message of her poem to the University of Cambridge sound as if it might have been issued from the pulpit. She had definite, if stereotyped, ideas that Heaven is a place of halos, angels, and reunion with God and His beloved; and she used these ideas with the same seriousness of purpose that surrounds her classical material. It is not at all strange that one who attended Boston's Old South Meeting House should show such firm Christian convictions and concern with the soul, and these facets of her personality made it very appropriate for friends to turn to her for elegies. In this vein we should not overlook her embellishment of Biblical accounts in her poems based on Isaiah and on the encounter of David and Goliath (following in an old New England tradition and beginning a long tradition of Negro writers' embellishing the Bible). In both of these poems she adds to the Biblical

11. *The Negro Author,* p. 24.
12. *Ibid.,* p. 27.
13. *Ibid.,* p. 373, *n.* 75.

narrative and couches it in the neoclassical form which was familiar to her from the poems she read most—iambic pentameter couplets, opening invocation of the muse, panoramic view, attempted elevation of language (especially in the august speeches of the characters), eye-catching details, and hyperbole.

It is clear that Phillis read as much as possible. However, her favorite volumes are reported to have been the Bible, a collection of tales from mythology, and Pope's Homer; and we also know that she read at least some of the Latin authors in the original. Although some of her subject matter can be traced to classical origins outside of Pope's translations and although it is difficult to pinpoint clearly indisputable instances of his influence on her, it still is held by all who study her poems that Pope's translation of Homer was the single most important influence on her work. To that view, I too subscribe.

Certainly Pope's relatively fixed formulas for neoclassical poetic music found a ready response in this young African girl's natural imitative ability. However, I suspect that what led her back to Pope time and time again was really Homer's grand narrative, which had retained its greatness of concept even when encased in a neoclassic gait. Phillis was content to take the form she found because she could use it with ease, but it seems that in choosing Niobe, Goliath, Lee, and Washington, she was also feeling the tug of Homer's heroes on her impressionable young mind. I believe it was the classical world which kindled her talent and interest, though she used the neoclassical approach because of its vogue, its availability to her, and her ability to employ it. Her best-treated subject matter tends to support this view. There has been conjecture about what the rising romanticism would have done to her work if she had lived either later or longer. However, one may with more pertinence wonder what her poems would have been like had she been immersed in Milton sooner, for what he had done seems to suit her basic interests more. Phillis Wheatley was not the wasp that Pope was, but tended to be more compatible with Milton's Christian classicism and its view of life. It is interesting to note that in a poem dated December 5, 1774, she acknowledges her proper place to be but at the feet of such men as Newton and Milton and reserves for Milton, the grand creator—not for Pope, the translator—the title "British Homer."

On the other hand, even in the face of these facts and of the fact that her best poems seem to be those which depart most from neoclassical imitation, the strong influence of neoclassicism on her in her first, formative years as a poet may not have been a bad thing. It certainly gave her a respect for regularity (which even Wordsworth recognized as necessary), happened to be something she had a natural talent to reproduce (thus probably encouraging her in her own eyes and in the eyes of those who made Pope so popular), was readily available, and was usually not too deep philosophically. The pity is that events and her short career did not really give her talent time to discover if it could broaden, mature, and diversify.

The neoclassical influence also may have been responsible for the fact that there is little about Phillis herself in her poems. She certainly leaves the reader of her poems only slightly aware of her being a Negro and a slave. Redding has pointed out, "The Wheatleys had adopted her, but she had adopted their terrific New England conscience."[14] She was conscious of her color, but the degree to which she became a New Englander helped moderate this awareness during her most formative years. For her, Heaven was more to be desired than earthly toil, not so much for the physical rewards which many later slaves would emphasize, but rather for its spiritual rewards. Redding seems to chide her for her

14. *To Make A Poet Black,* p. 9.

apparent unconcern over slavery in a Boston where it was obviously much discussed,[15] but it was probably better for her poetry that whatever feelings she had about this subject were sublimated.

What few thoughts on Africa and slavery's effect on her which are included in her poems are interesting. Her individual situation did not equip her for abolitionism—indeed her real and necessary poetic patron was her slave "master." She came to America too young for that experience not to be modified by her being part of the Wheatley household, and she did not live long enough or under such circumstances after leaving that household to turn her pen to or to feel the need for crusading. However, she clearly was not entirely unmindful of the Negro's delegated place in the popular mind of the time. She makes good use of this knowledge in her poems to the Earl of Dartmouth and to the University at Cambridge, almost turning it to advantage to strengthen her points. She surely was aware of the fact that much of her own notoriety was the result of her work's being always labeled as that of an African (and she is careful to so call herself in several poems and to entitle one poem "To S. M., A Young African Painter, On Seeing His Works").

In her particular case, she seems to have viewed the captivity which brought her to Boston and to the Wheatleys as certainly not entirely unfortunate. Her poem to Dartmouth speaks of "seeming cruel fate" which snatched her "from Afric's fancied happy seat," and she shows concern primarily for the sorrow of her parents. However, she immediately makes it clear that she does not endorse slavers, slavery, or the usual results of slavery. Her poem "On Being Brought From Africa to America" sees the event as fortunate because it allowed her to be a Christian, and the poem almost sounds like the product of missionary propaganda. It is in this same vein that she speaks to the students at the University

15. *Ibid.*, pp. 9-10.

at Cambridge of her not enjoying the advantages they have because of her having so recently come from a land of "errors" and "gloom," brought forth to safety by the "gracious hand" of God. On the other hand, in her poem dated December 5, 1774, to the "Gentleman in the Navy" she seems quite taken with western Africa as a place of peace, beauty, and plenty. However, this may be simply a reaction to his poem to which this is a reply. At any rate, in "To Maecenas" she makes it clear that she thinks the muses ought to come to her aid and not give Terence alone claim to being an inspired African poet. (Of course, here is reflected the narrowness of her knowledge.) Incidentally, this also affords us one of those few instances when we learn anything of Phillis herself from her poems.

Although she did not write much of slavery, certain of her poems do reflect an awareness of current events affecting the society in which she lived. For example, see her poems to the king and to the Earl of Dartmouth, and her later poems on Lee and Washington and the poem "Liberty and Peace." Incidentally, in each of these last three poems she refers to this land as "Columbia," and it has been claimed that she was the first to use the term with this meaning in print in America.[16]

In her worst poems, Phillis falls prey to the clichés of neoclassical poetic diction, to wrenched syntax, to trite devices, to run-away rhythm, and to an overemphasis on religion. These appear most frequently in her occasional verses. Over one-third of her extant poems are elegies. Loggins points out the long tradition of elegies in Boston and the fact that hers too are impersonal and artificial in feeling, with much use of hyperbole, overuse of personification, and pompousness of ornamentation.[17] Not only is neoclassical tradition to blame here, but also the fact that most of these

16. George H. Moore, "The Name 'Columbia,'" *Proceedings of the Massachusetts Historical Society,* Second Series, II (1885-86), 163.

17. *The Negro Author,* p. 22.

were written on request, to embellish the memory of the departed. Yet, sometimes a genuine note of understanding and concern is found in her elegies, especially for persons she knew, at which times one feels even more the strain resulting from her poetic form. Sometimes her good product is found close by her poor one in the same poem. In "To a Lady and Her Children, On the Death of Her Son and Their Brother," she speaks of the mother's realization of the death: "Th' unhappy mother sees the sanguine rill/Forget to flow, and nature's wheels stand still." However, later in the same poem we are rudely accosted by the cliché and the wrenched syntax of the following: "No more in briny show'rs, ye friends around,/Or bathe his clay, or waste them on the ground." However, in her better work, she is much more in control of the syntax and rhythm and employs them with unobjectionable diction and figures, if not always fresh or new ones. For example, note her poem "Thoughts on the Works of Providence," in which she speaks of dawn and sunset: "Or when the morning glows with rosy charms,/Or the sun slumbers in the ocean's arms," and speaks of God "Which round the sun revolves this vast machine,/Though to his eye its mass a point appears," and of the moon which "True to her course th' impetuous storm derides,/Triumphant o'er the winds, and surging tides." Or note the opening lines of "An Hymn to the Evening": "Soon as the sun forsook the eastern main/The pealing thunder shook the heav'nly plain;/Majestic grandeur! From the zephyr's wing,/Exhales the incense of the blooming spring./Soft purl the streams, the birds renew their notes,/And through the air their mingled music floats." These are not great lines, but they are good ones.

Of course, her favorite poetic form was the heroic couplet of English neoclassicism. All of her extant poems employ this, with five exceptions.[18] There are occasional interspersed

18. These exceptions are "On Virtue," which is free verse ending

three-line rhyme sequences, and "An Answer to the Rebus" departs from the heroic couplet in its last four lines to employ iambic tetrameter. She attempted her most complicated formal poetic pattern in "An Hymn to Humanity," a poor poem; but her one use of ballad stanza was quite successful. However, she apparently found that the heroic couplet came easier, and she did not abandon it in her later poems.

Phillis only occasionally used such devices as alliteration and onomatopoeia, and they were not significant in her poetic method. However, as with good neoclassicism, the caesura was important as she constantly attempted not just iambic pentameter couplets, but the heroic couplet employed by Alexander Pope. Unfortunately, her work was subject to the uncertainties and irregularities of eighteenth century English spelling and punctuation, and she was too dependent on elision for regulating her meter. She also rhymes in the eighteenth-century manner—*e.g.*, "join" with "divine." However, the era will not excuse her occasional lack of consistency in tense, especially noticeable in her poem on Goliath. If she were responsible for the order of the poems in the 1773 edition, we might note that that order is basically a good one. She seems to have preferred the medium length poem of from forty to fifty lines, with the eight-line "On Being Brought from Africa to America" being her shortest and her two narrative poems on Goliath and on Niobe being her longest, each having 224 lines. Incidentally, Miss Wheatley seldom employed her talents in narrative; but she was

---

with a heroic couplet (although she may have intended it for blank verse); "To the University of Cambridge, In New England," which is primarily blank verse; "Ode to Neptune," which has three sections of six lines each, with each section having four lines of iambic tetrameter couplets, followed by one heroic couplet; "An Hymn to Humanity," which has six sections of six lines each, with each section having first an iambic tetrameter couplet, followed by an iambic trimeter line, followed by an iambic tetrameter couplet, followed by an iambic trimeter line which rhymes with the third line of the section; and "A Farewell to America," which is in ballad stanza.

fairly good at it, sustaining the reader's interest with a good mixture of details, action, speech, and pacing.

For seven of her poems we have revised versions which show that she could improve the diction, poetic figures, syntax, rhythm, tone, rhyme, and general quality of her work through both changes and deletions. Would that she had done even more revision, but her imitative mind apparently did not have the temperament for extensively and consistently taking such pains. Also, what she produced gained adequate notoriety for the young slave girl, and her critical motives asked little more of her even though she admired the great writers she had encountered in her reading. Yet, such generalization may be unfair to her, because we have only two manuscripts of her work, each of which makes it clear that she revised it before publication. In every other instance when we have two editions of the same poem in her lifetime, it is clear that some revision took place between them. On the other hand, the examples of the improvements of which she was capable and the poor quality of some of the extant poems for which there is no evidence of rewriting lead one to retain the conviction that she probably did not revise all of her poems, certainly did not revise most of them much, and obviously should have revised more. The body of her work might also have been better if she had discarded a few of her works—but of what writer can that not be said to some degree, and where does one stop? Perhaps she did discard, though the evidence is against such a supposition.

Basically, Phillis was a spontaneous poet, not a laborious one. In view of this, the general regularity of her meter is striking. The poems for which we have evidence of revision are her poems on the deaths of Dr. Sewall, Mrs. Thankfull Leonard, Mrs. Pitkin, Mr. Leonard, and the Reverend Mr. Whitefield, and her poems to the university at Cambridge and on recollection. This evidence is all available to the reader for the first time in this edition of her work, and he may see the extent of it (little in most cases, much in a few) and judge its effect for himself. I believe he will find it generally favorable. However, it is uncertain what she learned from the process, for her later poems do not show a great improvement over some of her earlier ones. On the other hand, her career was sporadic, early, brief, and in its later stages difficult.

Nevertheless, in the community where she lived, Phillis practiced the art of poetry and was known there for that practice; and Boston in the years before and after the American Revolution was still the literary capital of America, as well qualified to produce, cultivate, encourage, and judge a poet as any community in the land. In part because she was young, in part because she was female, and in part because she was a Negro and nominally a slave, her work has too often been overpraised. On the other hand, she has also been too often dealt with unfairly or not at all because of this overpraising and what engendered it. The proper position lies somewhere between these usual extremes, for her work definitely does have some literary merit of its own, despite its obvious shortcomings. It becomes even more significant in any literary-historical consideration of it.

Her poems are certainly as good or better than those of most of the poets usually included and afforded fair treatment in a discussion of American poetry before 1800, and this same evaluation holds true when she is compared with most of the minor English poets of the eighteenth century who wrote in the neoclassical tradition. Finding our early literary soil generally unfit for real poetry, Moses Coit Tyler in his *A History of American Literature 1607-1765* and *The Literary History of the American Revolution* does, however, treat many "verse-writers," especially those of New England. In comparing his appraisals of these writers, as frank and blunt as the statements are, one still cannot help but conclude that his harsh treatment of Phillis Wheatley in the latter volume is unjust. For she certainly deserves as much praise, or as little blame (depending on whether one is measuring by a relative standard or by an absolute one, as Tyler was), as such early poets as Thomas Morton, Benjamin Tompson, Thomas Godfrey, Nathaniel Evans, Nathaniel Niles, Jonathan Odell, Joseph Stansbury, Michael Wigglesworth, Ebenezer Cook, Mather Byles,[19] and perhaps Francis Hopkinson, John Trumbull, Timothy Dwight, Joel Barlow, and Anne Bradstreet (though Phillis is not as sustained and consistent as these latter five, her best work certainly is worthy of inclusion with their best).[20] There is no doubt whatever that she was the best American Negro author before 1800 and the best American Negro poet until Frances Ellen Watkins Harper in the middle of the nineteenth century—some say the best until Dunbar at the end of that century.

As I have said, she was not a great poet; but in her way, in her time, and in her locale, she was a fairly good writer of poems generally in imitation of the neoclassical mode made popular by Alexander Pope. She deserves our consideration by either absolute or relative standards—and not just because of her youth, her sex, or her race. As Perry Miller and countless others have reminded us and shown us,

19. One becomes especially impatient with the treatment given Byles by various authors and editors because he offers such an apt comparison with Phillis. (See the Facsimile Text Society edition of Mather Byles, *Poems on Several Occasions,* with introduction by C. Lennart Carlson [New York, 1940]). Similarities extend to volume title, preface, general subject matter, age, and place (Boston, where his volume appeared in 1744). One has only to compare the poem which each has on the subject of David versus Goliath to note Phillis' superior imagination, sophistication, and general poetic ability. She is in command of her subject and is not just adapting a biblical account. Yet most general accounts of or collections of early American poetry certainly do not acknowledge her superiority to Byles.

20. See Tyler's two literary histories and most anthologies which include much pre-nineteenth century American poetry, including Frederick C. Prescott and Gerald D. Sanders, eds., *An Introduction to American Poetry* (New York, 1932).

it is indeed a mistake to think there is nothing worth reading in American literature before Washington Irving—and this applies to Negro authors as well, for there stands Phillis Wheatley of Boston, not one of the best, but far from one of the worst of the many who, in spite of the struggles of establishment, felt the influence of the muses in colonial America.

While this has been an attempt to give the reader a general introduction to Phillis Wheatley, there is at least one thing which has not been attempted which any person genuinely interested in her should be aware of. It has not given every fact which is known about her, but has given a reasonable account of her life and work, with emphasis on the proven facts. Certainly there are now available many elaborations of the brief biographical sketch given here. However, one finds in them many conflicting points, and apparently in some instances there has been extrapolation from the known facts because of the attractiveness of the subject.[21]

However, this young woman is of significance to us today almost solely because of her poems. Brawley has said, "Whoever now has a copy of this original [1773] edition [of Phillis Wheatley's poems] possesses the greatest treasure in the literature of the Negro."[22] The purpose of this edition is not only to make the poems of that first edition more readily available, but for the first time to bring together into one volume all of the extant poems and letters written by the young eighteenth-century Bostonian, Phillis Wheatley.

21. For example, Shirley Graham has written a whole book on the life of Phillis for children, *The Story of Phillis Wheatley* (New York: 1949), which contains relatively few proven facts, but is such a reasonable extrapolation that I am sure it gives the reader an appreciation and context which is not misleading. On the other hand, Martha Bacon in the first chapter of her *Puritan Promenade* (Boston, 1964) has taken a few facts and drawn highly questionable conclusions from them.

22. Benjamin Brawley, *Negro Builders and Heroes* (Chapel Hill, 1937), p. 21.

✦ *THE REPUTATION OF PHILLIS WHEATLEY, POET* ✦

For several obvious reasons, there has been a continuing, periodically emerging interest in Phillis Wheatley and her works since their first publication. Some indication of this can be seen in information given in the Introduction to this volume and in A Note on Text, particularly as it relates to republication. However, since there has never been much written concerning her reception through the decades, it seems appropriate to include in this volume not an exhaustive essay but an initial, selective although representative survey. This would enable her readers today to know something of her reputation since the 1770's, especially as most of the eighteenth- and nineteenth-century critiques are hard for the average reader to know of or to obtain—much less to see in some relation to one another.

A special interest in Phillis is first reflected in the note which usually appeared with her 1770 poem on Whitefield, pointing out that she was a "Servant Girl, of 17 years of age . . . but 9 Years in this country from Africa"; and though they were never of the very best quality, her poems were good enough soon to arouse the suspicions of those who did not know her. Therefore, a note to the public appears at the front of her volume of 1773 to assure the reader that these are indeed the work of Mrs. Wheatley's slave, Phillis. This note was signed by eighteen of "the most respectable characters in Boston, that none might have the least ground for disputing . . . ." The eighteen included the governor and lieutenant governor, seven ministers, and Mr. Wheatley.

Among the early tributes to Phillis was the second known poem by America's first published Negro poet, Jupiter Hammon. The poem, *An Address to Miss Phillis Wheatly* [sic], *Ethiopian Poetess, in Boston, who came from Africa at eight years of age, and soon became acquainted with the Gospel of Jesus Christ,* was published as a broadside dated Hartford, August 4, 1778. It was twenty-one stanzas of four lines each, printed in double column, at the end of which was an acknowledgment that the poem had been published "by the Author, and a number of his friends, who desire to join with him in their best regards to Miss Wheatly [*sic*]." Hammon admonishes her to thank God for all the special things God has done for her, and he suggests: "Come you, Phillis, now aspire,/And seek the living God,/So step by step thou mayst go higher,/Till perfect in the Word."

It is especially interesting to note how Phillis' poems have been treated by some of the reviewers for periodicals. The 1773 edition was very quickly reviewed by *The London Magazine: Or, Gentleman's Monthly Intelligencer,* a prominent periodical of the time which had published one of her poems in March of the preceding year. In the September, 1773, number (XLII, 456) it quite fairly said:

> These poems display no astonishing power of genius; but when we consider them as the production of a young untutored African, who wrote them after six months [*sic*] casual study of the English language and of writing, we cannot suppress our admiration of talents so vigorous and lively. We are the more surprised too, as we find her verses interspersed with the poetical names of the ancients, which she has in every instance used with strict propriety. As our readers may be curious enough to wish for a specimen of this Afric Muse's poetry, we subjoin the following ["Hymn to the Morning"].

This earliest known critical notice of her poems was one of the longer portions of that month's section of "An Impartial Review of New Publications."

In December of 1773, *The Monthly Review* of London was less concerned with the poems than with the fact that their author was a Negro slave, saying, among other things, the following (XLIX, 457-59):

> If we believed, with the ancient mythologists, that genius is the offspring of the sun, we should rather wonder that the sable race have not been more distinguished by it, than express our surprize at a single instance. . . .
>
> The poems written by this young negro bear no endemial marks of solar fire or spirit. They are merely imitative; and, indeed, most of those people have a turn for imitation, though they have little or none for invention. . . .
>
> She has written many good lines, and now and then one of superior character has dropped from her pen . . . .
>
> We are much concerned to find that this ingenious young woman is yet a slave. The people of Boston boast themselves chiefly on their principles of liberty. One such act as the purchase of her freedom, would, in our opinion, have done them more honor than hanging a thousand trees with ribbons and emblems.

This was a major review that month (not in the "Monthly Catalogue"), approximately one and one-half pages long, in the periodical which has been called "the earliest Review of importance in English literature."[1] (Of note are the review's reflections of the conflicts between England and the colonies and reflections of predominant stereotype ideas about Negroes.)

The 1834 *Memoir and Poems* brought forth more periodical notice (as well as a thirty-six page *Memoir of Phillis Wheatley* by B. B. Thatcher, published in Boston during the same year). On March 22, 1834, (IV, 47), *The Liberator*, an abolition weekly published in Boston, praised the memoir and reminded its readers of the prior publication of most

1. Walter Graham, *English Literary Periodicals* (New York, 1930), p. 209.

of the poems in its own pages. (Perhaps this publication of the poems by *The Liberator* had been partly responsible for the preparation of the 1834 volume.) It called Phillis the "famous African poetess" and said that her poems "are alike extraordinary, both as to their origin and merit; and deserve a place eminently conspicuous in every private and public library."

The New-England Magazine for April of 1834 carried a short notice of the *Memoir and Poems* in its "Literary Notices" section (VI, 344): "This is a republication from the earliest edition, which has now become very rare, of one of the most remarkable works, in some points of view, which the literary world have ever seen—the poems of an African Slave!" After a few more remarks, the notice ends with Phillis' hymn to the morning as a suitable example of "the literary character of these compositions . . . ."

In May of 1834, *The Christian Examiner,* a Unitarian magazine published in Boston, carried a five and one-half page review of the *Memoir and Poems.* "Contemporary and recent commentators agree that the *Christian Examiner* (1824-1869) contained some of the outstanding literary criticism in an American periodical during its four decades."[2] Charvat says that it "was the most important [American] magazine of the years 1830-1835. . . . Here was unitarianism at its intellectual best. Here too were the critical standards of the day warmed into life and vitality."[3] This particular review was written by William Joseph Snelling of Boston, a journalist, satirist, poet, author of books in prose, and later an editor of the *Boston Herald.* Snelling's review is honest and interesting, the product of both the reformer and the

2. Frances Pedigo, "Critical Opinions of Poetry, Drama, and Fiction, in the *Christian Examiner,* 1824-1869" (unpublished Ph.D. dissertation, University of North Carolina, 1953), p. 301.

3. William Charvat, *The Origins of American Critical Thought, 1810-1835* (New York, 1961), p. 198.

man of letters. Its first three and one-quarter pages are a summary of and comment on the memoirs; then:

> We turn to her poetry. It seems to us respectable, though not of a high order. Yet many of the white writers of this country have enjoyed a transient reputation on much less intrinsic merit! What proportion of the rhymesters, who enrich our newspapers and magazines with their effusions, can write half so well as Phillis Wheatley? She had no assistance. . . . Accordingly, we find some ill-constructed and harsh and prosaic lines, but not so many by half as in the verses of most of her contemporary American poets. That her lines are full of feeling, no one will deny who has read the extract we have already given. That she had considerable originality will be apparent from her epitaph on Dr. Sewall [which follows]. [XVI, 172.]
>
> Phillis Wheatley, we think, was a precocious genius, destined very rapidly to acquire a certain degree of excellence, and there to stop for ever [*sic*]. As mediocrity, or even moderate merit in song, is never tolerated, we dare not hope that her works will ever be very popular or generally read; for readers never take into account the disadvantages the writer may have labored under. It is not just that they should. . . . It is little consolation to him who has wasted his time and money in buying and reading a wretched production, to be told that it was written by an apprentice or a woman. We do not mean by this to express any disapprobation of the publication before us, but merely to say that, singular as its merits are, they are not of the kind that will command admiration. Still the work will live,—there will always be friends enough of liberty and of the cause of negro improvement not to let it sink into oblivion, and many will desire to possess it as a curiosity. . . . As a friend of the African and of mankind at large, we are happy to record our tribute of praise in behalf of one who was an honor and ornament to her race and her kind. [P. 174.]

Among the other things he says, Snelling concludes that "In the midst of obloquy attached to her hue, she reached an intellectual eminence known to few of the females of that day, and not common even now" (p. 174). The most important thing about this review is its appearance. However, while it is sympathetic, it does find her poetry wanting when judged against absolute standards.

A fourth review of the *Memoir and Poems* appeared in New York in *The Knickerbocker* in August of 1834. It was a ten and one-half page, unsigned, lead article, entitled "African Anecdotes." It begins: "This is a timely republication of a work [the poems], which has now become so rare, even among the bibliopoles, that it is much to be doubted whether half a dozen copies of it might be found in the country" (IV, 85). After dealing with several other matters, the reviewer comments on the poems:

> The style of the poems is evidently formed, in a great degree, after that of Pope, a writer now in the golden age of his fame; and, indeed, we not unfrequently meet with passages which remind us of the model so closely, that we cannot but think the original editor or printer failed to do the writer the common justice of attaching the usual marks of quotation to matter, here and there, that has very much the air of an extract. [A few lines of the "Address to Imagination" are quoted.]
>
> These lines . . . indicate, perhaps as sufficiently as any thing we can either cite or say, the cultivation of her literary taste and the development of her poetical genius. It must, of course, be remembered under what circumstances she commenced her career [elaborated for five lines]. While passages of her productions, then are characterized by the beautiful and even sublime expression of fine thoughts, and while they are distinguished throughout by an eminent degree of that harmony for which her race are supposed to have a peculiar sensibility, it is surely to be wondered at, if, on the whole, they should rather suggest to the philosophical mind what human, and what African nature is, and what it may accomplish under certain problematical circumstances, than furnish an intrinsic

> gratification to the mature taste, or a luxury to the mere lover of poetry. [P. 91.]

He then speaks of the anecdotes about the inspired nature of the writing of the poems and cites "the artlessness, in one sense of the word, which is for the most part a recommendation of the poems." This artlessness he speaks of further, not in a derogatory way, as being the result of the poetess' lack of training, so that she "merely *enjoyed,* rather than *employed,* her inventive faculties" (p. 92). Approximately one page of the whole review is devoted to the poems. This review, also, finds the poems wanting; yet it is willing to couch its few passing remarks of praise in very complimentary terms. The review is almost too apologetic, and yet the book was chosen for review in a prominent place in the magazine, primarily for its biographical-sociological interests. Indeed, it has been contended that this book may have been reviewed because of an absence of abolition sentiment in the poems at a time when generally few works by Negro authors were being reviewed by major American magazines.[4] After all, the work reviewed presented posthumously the poems of a female Negro author with some reputation, whose views generally were not in conflict with those of conservative minds, while her deeds and demonstrated intellect appealed to the more liberal minds of the time.

During the abolition decades, Phillis Wheatley, of course, was often brought up in publications and discussions by both sides. There was also significant interest in her on the part of the Massachusetts Historical Society during the 1860's, which resulted most importantly in the printing of a poem, some letters, and other items pertinent to her (including Nathaniel B. Shurtleff's short memoir of Phillis, reprinted from the *Boston Daily Advertiser* of December 21,

4. Julian D. Mason, Jr., "The Critical Reception of American Negro Authors in American Magazines, 1800-1885" (unpublished Ph.D. dissertation, University of North Carolina, 1962), pp. 64-65.

1863) in its *Proceedings* (see page 97 and the appendix to this volume). The letters were also separately printed in 1864.

In July of 1884, a fifteen-page article on Phillis by Father John R. Slattery of St. Joseph's Seminary in Baltimore appeared in *The Catholic World*[5] as a sequel to his earlier article on the Negro mathematician, Benjamin Banneker. Most of the article is biographical, but some of it deals with her writing, and there is frequent extensive quotation of her poetry. At one point he says, "The reader will be astonished, no doubt, that a slave-girl should write so many poems from the fifteenth to the twentieth year of her age—a time of life when most girls are given to all giddiness. The lofty sentiments of her mind are still more wonderful when Phillis' race is remembered" (p. 495).

On March 6, 1897, *The Literary Digest* of New York carried an item entitled "Negro Poets" (XIV, 550-51), which had been generated by the recent publication of a volume of verse by Paul Dunbar. The article calls attention to the fact that John Edward Bruce had written in the Boston *Evening Transcript* about Negro writers before Dunbar. Bruce is quoted:

> The first negro poet to attract the attention of the American public, and whose genius and cleverness won her an international reputation and the friendship of the most distinguished people of her day, on both sides of the Atlantic, was Phillis Wheatly [*sic*]. . . . No article on negro poets would be complete without some reference to the remarkable young woman, who in that early day did so much to destroy the general impression that the negro was incapable of the higher intellectual development. [P. 550.]

However, from the beginning of her notoriety, attention to Phillis was by no means limited to periodicals. She was cited by numerous writers. Benjamin Rush in 1773 spoke of her: "There is now in the town of Boston a Free Negro

5. "Phillis Wheatley, The Negro Poetess," XXXIX, 484-98.

Girl [*sic*], about 18 years of age, who has been but 9 [*sic*] years in the country, whose singular genius and accomplishments are such as not only do honor to her sex, but to human nature. Several of her poems have been printed, and read with pleasure by the public."[6] This was probably before the 1773 volume of poems appeared, but Rush apparently continued his good opinions after seeing the 1773 volume.[7] (Notice that Phillis listed a letter to Dr. Rush in the proposal for her second book.) Voltaire, in a 1774 letter to Baron Constant de Rebecq, said of her: "Fontenelle avait tort de dire qu'il n'y aurait jamais de poëtes chez les Nègres: l y a actuellement une Négresse qui fait de très-bons vers anglais."[8]

Another who was ready to say there had never been a Negro poet was Thomas Jefferson, who included Phillis in the contention; but he also was answered. When he published his *Notes on Virginia* in 1784, "Query XIV" contained the following:

> Misery is often the parent of the most affecting touches in poetry. Among the blacks is misery enough, God knows, but no poetry. Love is the peculiar oestrum of the poet. Their love is ardent, but it kindles the senses only, not the imagination. Religion, indeed, has produced a Phyllis Whately [*sic*]; but it could not produce a poet. The compositions published under her name are below the dignity of criticism. The heroes of the Dunciad are to her, as Hercules to the author of that poem.[9]

(George Washington had been more generous. See his letter

6. *An Address To The Inhabitants of the British Settlements In America, Upon Slave-Keeping* (Boston, 1773), p. 2 *n.*

7. See William Dickson, *Letters on Slavery* (London, 1789), pp. 76-77, 187.

8. Quoted in Edward Derbyshire Seeber, *Anti-Slavery Opinion in France During the Second Half of the Eighteenth Century* (Baltimore, 1937), p. 57, *n.* 54.

9. *The Writings of Thomas Jefferson,* ed. Albert Ellery Bergh (Washington, 1907), II, 196.

in Part Two of this volume.) Gilbert Imlay defended Phillis against Jefferson's charge:

> I will transcribe part of her Poem on Imagination, and leave you to judge whether it is poetical or not. It will afford you an opportunity, if you have never met with it, of estimating her genius and Mr. Jefferson's judgment; and I think, without any disparagement to him, that by comparison, Phillis appears much the superior. Indeed, I should be glad to be informed what white upon this continent has written more beautiful lines. [Followed by 20 lines of the poem.][10]

In 1808, in his *De la littérature des nègres,* the noted Frenchman, Henri Grégoire, very much regretted that such an esteemed man as Jefferson had made such remarks.[11] In his account of Phillis, he says that he will refute Jefferson with the judgment of the public as shown by the publication of the 1773 volume and with its contents themselves, several of which he includes.[12] In 1810, Samuel Stanhope Smith, president of the College of New-Jersey and a member of the American Philosophical Society, declared, "But I will demand of Mr. Jefferson, or any other man who is acquainted with American planters, how many of those masters could have written poems equal to those of Phillis Whately [*sic*]?"[13]

In 1878, Jefferson's remarks were still reverberating, and in the November-December, 1878, issue of *The North American Review* there was an article by James Parton entitled "Antipathy to the Negro." In the course of the article Parton mentions Jefferson's views on Negro creativity and then continues:

10. *A Topographical Description of The Western Territory of North America* (New York, 1793), I, 185-86.

11. *An Enquiry Concerning The Intellectual and Moral Faculties, And Literature of Negroes & Mulattoes, Distinguished in Science, Literature And The Arts,* transl. D. B. Warden (Brooklyn, 1810), pp. 44-45.

12. *Ibid.,* pp. 236-37, 238-41.

13. *An Essay on the Causes of the Variety of Complexion and Figure in the Human Species* (New-Brunswick and New York, 1810), p. 269 *n.*

> It was this passage in his "Notes on Virginia" that appears to have led a French author (M. Grégoire) to compile a work, in 1808, on the "Literature of the Negroes," a copy of which he sent to Mr. Jefferson during his presidency. . . . Unfortunately the bishop's book possessed no value, because he omitted to ascertain whether his literary negroes were of pure or mixed blood and his desire to make out a case for the Negro made him blindly credulous. The colored poet, Phillis Wheatley, had her admirers a hundred years ago in Boston, where her volume can still occasionally be found. We have carefully looked over it, and cannot deny the justice of Jefferson's remarks upon it. She was a poet very much as "Blind Tom" is a musician, her verses being the merest echo of the common jingle of her day. . . . A fatal facility of imitation stands in the way of this interesting race, and we cannot fairly deny that facts give support to the opinion of an inherent mental inferiority. It is ninety years since Jefferson published his "Notes," and we cannot yet name one negro of pure blood who has taken the first, the second, the third, or the tenth rank in business, politics, art, literature, scholarship science, or philosophy. To the present hour the negro has contributed nothing to the intellectual resources of man . . . . [CXXVII, 487-88.]

In July of 1880, *The National Quarterly Review* had a twenty-six-page review article by R. T. Greener, the first Negro to graduate from Harvard College (1870), where he had won the Boylston Prize in oratory twice and the Bowdoin Prize for a dissertation.[14] Parton's article, Jefferson's writings, and Grégoire's book were reviewed together for the primary purpose of pointing out the ignorance of most Americans concerning the accomplishments of Negroes. In the process, he cites Imlay's remarks concerning Phillis (LXI, 173-74). (Of course, Greener was not the first Negro to refute Jefferson's views of the abilities of Negroes, but his was one

14. For a summary of the various achievements of this distinguished gentleman, see Richard Bardolph, *The Negro Vanguard* (New York, 1959), p. 88; or the *Dictionary of American Biography*.

of the more urbane of the written refutations and one which was assured of a somewhat unique audience.)

Some other eighteenth- and nineteenth-century acknowledgments of Phillis and her poems (usually favorable) are to be found in: Thomas Clarkson, *An Essay on the Slavery and Commerce of the Human Species, Particularly the Africans* (London, 1788) (*e.g.*, p. 122: ". . . this observation, that if the authoress *was designed for slavery*, . . . the greater part of the inhabitants of Britain must lose their claim to freedom.") ; Thomas Branagan, *A Preliminary Essay, On the Oppression Of the Exiled Sons of Africa* (Philadelphia, 1804) (*e.g.*, p. 102: "Are not her poetical compositions . . . excellent, not only for their piety, but their poetical beauties?"); Joseph Brown Ladd, "The Prospects of America" (a poem in which she is praised along with Freneau and Barlow), *The Literary Remains of Joseph Brown Ladd,* compiled by Elizabeth Haskins (New York, 1832), p. 35; Lydia M. Child, *An Appeal In Favor of That Class of Americans Called Africans* (Boston, 1833), p. 171; Abigail Mott, *Biographical Sketches and Interesting Anecdotes of Persons of Color* (New York, 1838) , pp. 15-18; *Chambers' Miscellany of Useful and Entertaining Tracts* (Edinburgh, 1846), Vol. VII, No. 63; Caroline May, *The American Female Poets* (Philadelphia, 1848), p. 39; *Wheatley, Banneker, and Horton* (Boston, 1849), compiled by William G. Allen, containing a memoir of Phillis, a number of her poems, and Washington's letter to her: Evert A. and George L. Duyckinck, *Cyclopedia of American Literature* (New York, 1856), I, 368 (*e.g.*, favorably compares her with Anne Bradstreet and says she is a respectable follower of Pope); Benjamin J. Lossing, *Eminent Americans* (New York, 1881) (she is one of the few women treated); Justin Winsor, ed., *The Memorial History of Boston* (Boston, 1881), III, 147, and IV, 339; Phebe A. Hanaford, *Daughters of America* (Boston, 1883) p. 37; Edmund Clarence Stedman and Ellen M. Hutchinson, eds., *A Library of American Literature From the Earliest Settlement to the Present Time* (New York, 1892), Vol. III; Charles F. Richardson, *American Literature 1607-1885* (New York, 1895), II, 9 (*e.g.*: "Some of the poems are of decided excellence; good lines of the prevalent 'classic' style are not hard to find; the general merit of the [1773] collection easily surpasses that of Mrs. Bradstreet's; and when we make allowance for its artificiality, we may readily admit that it equals the average first volume of poems to-day. . . . The book remains the principal literary achievement of the colored race in America."); Katherine Lee Bates, *American Literature* (New York, 1898), p. 79; and S. Austin Allibone, *A Critical Dictionary of English Literature and British and American Authors* (Philadelphia, 1899), III, 2666. Phillis is, of course, also treated by almost every Negro author writing about the achievements of his race, including, from the nineteenth century, William C. Nell, R. B. Lewis, William Wells Brown, George Washington Williams, and Frederick Douglass.[15]

The above listing is by no means exhaustive, but only additionally illustrative of the continuing interest in and reputation of Phillis Wheatley and her poems on through the nineteenth century into the present one. This fluctuating reputation continues in the twentieth century, but it has suffered from regrettable neglect in at least two instances: Phillis is not even mentioned in *The Cambridge History of American Literature* or in the *Literary History of the United States*.[16] In these she deserves only the meager treatment of a minor author, but she definitely deserves that, along with the scores of other minor authors of comparable ability and reputation who do appear. A similar claim can be leveled

15. Consult Vernon Loggins, *The Negro Author* (New York, 1931), for titles, etc. Loggins also has a good section on Phillis.

16. However, in the bibliography of the latter, volume III, page 100, there is a single sentence: "The Negro poetaster Phillis Wheatley (*ca.* 1753-1784) achieved something of a vogue with the publication of her *Poems of Various Subjects* (1773), though it received little critical notice."

at many of our contemporary anthologies of the early period of our literature which omit any mention of Phillis Wheatley, who was recognized by her contemporaries as at least a little bit of light in that literarily dreary and weak period when our literature necessarily suffered while major concern and effort were turned to establishing a nation.

In the twentieth century, for various reasons, there has been more attention paid to our Negro authors per se, and Phillis has shared in this appropriately. However, the foremost method of praising an author is to keep his works available through reprinting. Along with the sincere but more limited efforts of those many others who have made either most or a few of her poems available to the readers of the twentieth century, this volume also shares in the tradition of praise through republication.

✦ *A NOTE ON TEXT* ✦

As is clear from the table of contents and from the arrangement of the volume, the main body of this edition is Phillis Wheatley's 1773 *Poems on Various Subjects, Religious and Moral.* The poems and frontmatter (excluding the separate page with the line "Entered at Stationers Hall" and the frontispiece—see below) of that volume have been printed here in the order in which they appear in a copy of that first edition (with pages the size they were before they were cut to standard publication size) which is in the Rare Book Room of the Louis Round Wilson Library of The University of North Carolina at Chapel Hill (which copy correlates with a copy of the first edition—with the pages cut to standard publication size—in the Rare Book Room of the Duke University Library).

The capitalization, punctuation, spelling, italics, and general format of that same edition have been preserved in this one. Though they are in one sense imperfect, they represent the most textually authentic representation of these poems published during the lifetime of the author and do not present problems which hinder the reader and his understanding of and appreciation of the poems which are great enough to offset the partially retained "flavor" of eighteenth-century publishing. However, the eighteenth-century printed *s* resembling very much the printed *f* has not been retained, the "tag word" appearing at the bottom of each page anticipating the first word of the next page has not been retained, and the beginning of each poem does not appear at the top of a fresh page as in the original. In other words, this is by no means a facsimile of the 1773 edition, although there was a conscious effort, by basing this one on that first edition, to give the reader an experience more like that of the original eighteenth-century readers than has any of the other republications.

Apparently the first of these republications came in London in 1773, for the 1917 *American Book Prices Current* lists a "Second Edition, corrected," called *Poems on Comic, Serious and Moral Subjects,* as having been sold by Charles F. Heartman in New York in 1916 for $51. Heartman includes a photocopy of the title page in his *Phillis Wheatley (Phillis Peters): A Critical Attempt and a Bibliography of Her Writings* (New York, 1915). He says that the contents are the same as the 1773 edition. (No one that I know of has been able to find a copy of this "second" edition. However, there apparently is a 1787 London edition with the same title and claim in the Schomburg Collection of the New York Public Library. See the *Dictionary Catalog of the Schomburg Collection of Negro Literature and History* [Boston, 1962], IX, 8250.) Definitely known republications were: Philadelphia, 1786 (first American edition) 1787, and 1789; Albany, 1793; Philadelphia, 1801, as an addendum to volume two of the translation from the French of Joseph Lavallee's *The Negro Equalled by Few Europeans*; Walpole, New Hampshire, 1802; Hartford, 1804; Halifax, 1814, as an addendum to *The Interesting Narrative of The Life of Olaudah Equiano, or Gustavus Vassa, The African*; New England, 1816; in a volume with a memoir of Phillis by Margaretta Matilda Odell, published in Boston in 1834, 1835, and 1838;[1]

1. The 1838 volume also contains poems by George Moses Horton at the end. The *Memoir and Poems* in the 1830's stirred new interest in Phillis Wheatley and her poems, and may have been inspired by the periodic reprinting of her poems in *The Liberator* in 1832. It was probably the *Memoir and Poems* that the sixteen-year old Charlotte Forten (herself destined for a remarkable role in establishing the ability of the Negro in America) referred to in her journal on Friday, April 28, 1854: "This evening read 'Poems of Phillis Wheatly [*sic*],' an Afri-

and in Denver in 1887, with memoirs by W. H. Jackson. The poems of the 1773 volume (and some of the others) also appear in: *The Poems of Phillis Wheatley,* Philadelphia, 1909; *Phillis Wheatley (Phillis Peters): Poems and Letters,* edited by Charles F. Heartman, with an appreciation by Arthur Schomburg, New York (1915?); *Life and Works of Phillis Wheatley,* by G. Herbert Renfro, Washington, 1916; and *The Poems of Phillis Wheatley, edited with an Introduction and Notes by Charlotte Ruth Wright,* Philadelphia, 1930. Also, most of the poems of the 1773 volume were printed, one at a time, in *The Liberator* between February 11, 1832, and December 22, 1832 (not during 1831, as Loggins says).

While I have taken cognizance of these republications and the editing in them, they have not been used as a basis for the texts of the poems in this volume. Instead, I have always used the 1773 version, except for the poems in Part Two (see discussion below). It is possible that Phillis could have seen this work through the press while she was in London in 1773, even though it seems apparent that the book had little to do with her reasons or times for leaving and returning. There is clear evidence in this volume (see the Introduction and Part Two) that several of the poems included were revised for this publication, and we know from Wheatley's letter to the publisher dated November 14, 1772,

---

can slave, who lived in Boston at the time of the Revolution. She was a wonderfully gifted woman, and many of her poems are very beautiful. Her character and genius afford a striking proof of the falseness of the assertion made by some that hers is an inferior race. . . ." (*A Free Negro in the Slave Era: The Journal of Charlotte L. Forten* [New York, 1961], p. 55). The 1838 edition was apparently reissued in 1863. The *Proceedings of the Massachusetts Historical Society,* VII (1863-64), 270, *n.,* tells of "the issue at this time of some copies remaining on hand of what is called the 'third edition' . . . which had been published in 1838"; and on page 276, *n.,* further information is given about these "some two hundred copies" brought out, not by the publisher of the "third edition" of the *Memoir and Poems,* but by the publisher of the first and second editions of the same, which he had pieced together from printing done by both publishers.

that some part of a plan to publish the poems was underway that early. Phillis' poem in farewell to America is dated Boston, May 7, 1773,[2] and the dedication to the volume is dated Boston, June 12, 1773. These two (even allowing for the speculation of some that Phillis was already in England by June 12) give us a relatively certain period for her departure for England. The picture in the 1773 volume bears an inscription indicating publication on September 1, 1773 (however, see below regarding the picture), and the book was reviewed in *The London Magazine* in September. These give us a point after which we know publication had taken place, even though her letters seem to indicate that copies were not received in America until several months later and the *Boston Gazette* on January 24, 1774, advertised the book as "This Day Published" with an "Excellent Engraving of the Author" and advised subscribers to pick up their copies. Her letter to Obour Tanner of October 30, 1773, finds her back in America, probably since only a few weeks at the most. In short, the available evidence points to her either directly or indirectly having assented to the form of the poems as they appear in the 1773 volume (with the last known revisions before her death), thus making it the most authoritative, if not the most pleasing, textual source. Therefore, it has been followed in this volume (except, of course, for Part Two, which has a distinctly different purpose of its own).

The frontispiece of Phillis which appears in this edition is a copy of the one in the 1773 edition in the Wilson Li-

2. It is interesting to note how many of her poems we are able to date from dates or information given with or in them. Her earliest clearly dated poem (though not her first published and perhaps not her first written) was the one to the "University of Cambridge, in New-England." written in 1767, only six years after she came to this country. (However, see my note to her poem "To a Gentleman on his Voyage to Great-Britain," page 41 of this volume). Twenty of her forty-six poems (not counting revisions as separate poems) can be dated within the year and often closer than that.

brary in Chapel Hill, which was tipped-in after the original printing. This is especially evident in that the page bearing it in the copy at Chapel Hill is smaller than the other, uncut pages in that volume and is the same size as the cut pages in the 1773 edition at Duke University (which also has the frontispiece tipped-in facing the title page, where it is the same size as the other pages). There is an interesting note concerning this picture in *The Historical Magazine,* published in New York, for June, 1858 (II, 178-79), signed "J. H. T." It states: "In a letter from Mrs. Susannah Wheatley to Samson Occom, dated at Boston, March 29, 1773, is the following notice of the reception which the Countess of Huntingdon gave these poems, and of the way in which 'Phillis' picture' came to be prefixed to the first edition." After a few explanatory remarks, the note continues its quotation from Mrs. Wheatley's letter to the effect that she has received a letter from "Capt. Calef," whom she is expecting "every day" to arrive from England and whom her "son intends to go home with" (apparently referring to the upcoming visit of Nathaniel Wheatley to England, with Phillis accompanying him). Mrs. Wheatley then quotes from Captain Calef's letter, dated January 5:

> Mr. Bell (the printer) acquaints me that, about five weeks ago, he waited upon the Countess of Huntingdon with the poems, who was greatly pleas'd with them, and pray'd him to read them; and often would break in upon him, and say, "Is not this, or that, very fine? Do read another," and question'd him much, whether she was *real,* without a deception? He then convinced her by bringing my name in question. She is expected in Town in a short time, when we are both to wait upon her. I had like to forget to mention to you, she is fond of having the book dedicated to her; but one thing she desir'd which she said she hardly thought would be denied her, that was, to have Phillis' picture in the frontispiece. So that if you would get it done, it can be engraved here. I do imagine it

> can be easily done, and think would contribute greatly to the sale of the book. I am impatient to hear what the old Countess says upon the occasion, and shall take the earliest opportunity of waiting upon her when she comes to town.

We may have here a clue to the inclusion of both the testimonial letter to the public and the picture. It is also interesting to note the involvement in the publication proceedings on the part of Calef and of Mrs. Wheatley (probably because of her involvement in projects with Occom and the consequent associations with various people of note in England). The circumstances revealed by this letter and by the fact that the frontispiece was tipped-in suggest that the volume was printed approximately during the months when Phillis was in England and the frontispiece added as soon as it was available. Final publication then was dependent on the availability of the frontispiece; and from its bearing the date of September 1, we can presume the picture did not arrive soon enough for completion of the volume for distribution before Phillis felt compelled to return to Boston. (Perhaps she brought the picture with her. Mrs. Wheatley is reported to have had a picture of Phillis in Boston while Phillis was in England. The question arises whether the position in the 1773 volume of her poem to Scipio Moorhead with two other poems written in 1773 offers a suggestion as to the artist of her portrait.) Would that the originals of Mrs. Wheatley's and Captain Calef's letters were available.

The sources for the material in Part Two and the appendix are given with each item. (There one also will find information about the various reprintings of the 1770 poem on the death of Whitefield.) Part Two and the appendix endeavor to present all extant items definitely known to have been written by Phillis which were not included in the 1773 *Poems On Various Subjects,* including variants of poems (but it does not include items only suspected to have been by her, *e.g.,* the poem on the birthday of Pompey Stockbridge). In each case, the earliest source has been used as a basis for this edition. (It is interesting to note how she changed the titles of certain poems to make them less personal for the 1773 book.) The order of material in Part Two is chronological in terms of composition (as far as we know it) except that the poem on General Lee was put last because it was published very late (although written much earlier).

All notes in the present volume which are indicated by asterisks appeared in the sources used for this edition, and it is not known whether they were Phillis' notes or the printer's (though I think they were hers). The numbered notes are by the present editor. An attempt has been made through the notes to elucidate those items which the average reader might find difficulty in informing himself about, always with a primary goal of more clearly relating Phillis, her work, and her times. Ordinarily, information that can readily be found in generally available reference sources, such as general or classical dictionaries, has not been noted.

One wishes that Phillis' papers and manuscripts had been preserved, especially since there is clear evidence of her having written poems we do not have. However, it is reported that her husband confiscated her papers and other belongings, and we do not know what became of them. (We know that after her death at least one of her treasured books was sold to pay her husband's debts. It was the copy of *Paradise Lost* given to her by Mr. Brook Watson in London in July, 1773, which date helps confirm her presence in London at the time cited above. The volume is now in the library at Harvard.) It is to be hoped that a few additional valid items may turn up yet. Until then, this edition of the poems of Phillis Wheatley is the most complete, and hopefully the best, one available.

✦ *ACKNOWLEDGMENTS* ✦

Grateful acknowledgment is given to the following for permission to use the indicated items in this edition: The Louis Round Wilson Library of The University of North Carolina at Chapel Hill for the complete 1773 *Poems on Various Subjects,* including the picture of Phillis Wheatley; the American Antiquarian Society for the manuscript versions of "To the University of Cambridge, wrote in 1767—" and "On the Death of the rev'd Dr. Sewall. 1769.—"; the heirs of Charles F. Heartman (and to his sources, indicated in the notes to the poems) for broadside versions of the poem on the death of Whitefield, *"To Mrs.* Leonard, *on the Death of her* Husband," "To the Rev. Mr. *Pitkin* on the Death of his LADY," and *"To the Hon'ble* Thomas Hubbard, *Esq; On the Death of Mrs.* Thankfull Leonard"; the Henry E. Huntington Library and Art Gallery for a broadside version of the poem on the death of Whitefield; the Massachusetts Historical Society for "An Elegy, To Miss Mary Moorhead . . . ," the elegy on the death of Dr. Samuel Cooper, the poem on General Lee, the letters to Obour Tanner and the Earl of Dartmouth, and the proposals for a second volume of poems; The New-York Historical Society for "Liberty and Peace"; and Benjamin Quarles and *The Journal of Negro History* for the letter to the Rev. Mr. Samuel Hopkins.

Acknowledgment should also be given for the kind assistance of the staff of the library of The University of North Carolina at Chapel Hill (especially those of the Rare Book Room and the Interlibrary Center); for the willingness of a number of libraries and societies in various parts of the country to lend books or furnish photocopies of materials; for a grant from the Smith Fund of The University of North Carolina at Chapel Hill for assistance with obtaining materials; for funds provided by the William A. Whitaker Foundation for purchasing the 1773 edition of *Poems on Various Subjects* for the Wilson Library; for the scholarly publications of Dorothy Porter, Vernon Loggins, and Justin Winsor, which helped so much; for patience, understanding, and help from the staff and Board of Governors of The University of North Carolina Press; and for patience and help on the part of both my office staff and my family.

P O E M S

ON

VARIOUS SUBJECTS,

RELIGIOUS AND MORAL.

BY

PHILLIS WHEATLEY,

NEGRO SERVANT to Mr. JOHN WHEATLEY, of BOSTON, in NEW ENGLAND.

L O N D O N:

Printed for A. BELL, Bookseller, Aldgate; and sold by Messrs. COX and BERRY, King-Street, *BOSTON.*

MDCCLXXIII.

Part One

✤✤✤✤✤✤✤

Poems on Various Subjects, Religious and Moral

DEDICATION.

To the Right Honourable the

COUNTESS OF HUNTINGDON,[1]

THE FOLLOWING

POEMS

Are moſt reſpectfully

Inſcribed,

By her much obliged,

Very humble,

And devoted Servant,

Phillis Wheatley.

Boſton, June 12,
1773.

1. Selina Hastings (1707-1791), quite interested in the methodist movement and in literature. (See the Introduction and A Note on Text to this volume, the poems on Whitefield [p. 66] and to the Earl of Dartmouth [p. 33], and the "Proposals" for a second book [p. 112].)

PREFACE.

THE following POEMS were written originally for the Amuſement of the Author, as they were the Products of her leiſure Moments. She had no Intention ever to have publiſhed them; nor would they now have made their Appearance, but at the Importunity of many of her beſt, and moſt generous Friends; to whom ſhe conſiders herſelf, as under the greateſt Obligations.[2]

As her Attempts in Poetry are now ſent into the World, it is hoped the Critic will not ſeverely ſenſure their Defects; and we preſume they have too much Merit

to

2. This is a traditional "protest." It is probably true that she did not originally write with publication in mind, and her friends probably did suggest publication to her and even attempt it without her permission. However, five of these poems had already been published at someone's initiative, though in versions which she had since improved.

to be caſt aſide with Contempt, as worthleſs and trifling Effuſions.

As to the Diſadvantages ſhe has laboured under, with Regard to Learning, nothing needs to be offered, as her Maſter's Letter in the following Page will ſufficiently ſhew the Difficulties in this Reſpect ſhe had to encounter.

With all their Imperfections, the Poems are now humbly ſubmitted to the Peruſal of the Public.

The

The following is a Copy of a LETTER ſent by the Author's Maſter to the Publiſher.

PHILLIS was brought from *Africa* to *America*, in the Year 1761, between Seven and Eight Years of Age. Without any Aſſiſtance from School Education, and by only what ſhe was taught in the Family, ſhe, in ſixteen Months Time from her Arrival, attained the Engliſh Language, to which ſhe was an utter Stranger before, to ſuch a Degree, as to read any, the moſt difficult Parts of the Sacred Writings, to the great Aſtoniſhment of all who heard her.

As to her WRITING, her own Curioſity led her to it; and this ſhe learnt in ſo ſhort a Time, that in the Year 1765, ſhe wrote a Letter to the Rev. Mr. OCCOM, the *Indian* Miniſter, while in *England*.

She has a great Inclination to learn the Latin Tongue, and has made ſome Progreſs in it. This Relation is given by her Maſter who bought her, and with whom ſhe now lives.

JOHN WHEATLEY.

Boſton, Nov. 14, 1772.

To the PUBLICK.

AS it has been repeatedly suggested to the Publisher, by Persons, who have seen the Manuscript, that Numbers would be ready to suspect they were not really the Writings of PHILLIS, he has procured the following Attestation, from the most respectable Characters in *Boston*, that none might have the least Ground for disputing their *Original*.

WE whose Names are under-written, do assure the World, that the POEMS specified in the following Page, * were (as we verily believe) written by PHILLIS, a young Negro Girl, who was but a few Years since, brought an uncultivated Barbarian from *Africa*, and has ever since been, and now is, under the Disadvantage of serving as a Slave in a Family in this Town. She has been examined by some of the best Judges, and is thought qualified to write them.[3]

His Excellency THOMAS HUTCHINSON, *Governor*,

The Hon. ANDREW OLIVER, *Lieutenant-Governor*.

The Hon. Thomas Hubbard,
The Hon. John Erving,
The Hon. James Pitts,
The Hon. Harrison Gray,
The Hon. James Bowdoin,
John Hancock, *Esq*;
Joseph Green, *Esq*;
Richard Carey, *Esq*;

The Rev. Charles Chauncy, *D. D.*
The Rev. Mather Byles, *D. D.*
The Rev Ed. Pemberton, *D. D.*
The Rev. Andrew Elliot, *D.D.*
The Rev. Samuel Cooper, *D.D.*
The Rev. Mr. Samuel Mather,
The Rev. Mr. John Moorhead,
Mr. John Wheatley, *her Master*.

N. B. The original Attestation, signed by the above Gentlemen, may be seen by applying to *Archibald Bell*, Bookseller, No. 8, *Aldgate-Street*.

---

* The Words "*following Page*," allude to the Contents of the Manuscript Copy, which are wrote at the Back of the above Attestation.

3. Information is given about Oliver, Hubbard, Bowdoin, Cooper, and Moorhead with poems concerning them or members of their households, which see. Hutchinson was governor of Massachusetts at the time, but is more noted as an historian. Erving was a prominent Boston merchant. Gray and Hancock were quite active merchants. Green was known as merchant, poet, and wit. Chauncey was pastor of the First Unitarian Church and a respected author on religious subjects, particularly noted for his stand against Whitefield and emotional religion. Byles was not only a minister, but was known also for his poetry and wit. Samuel Mather, pastor of the Tenth Congregational Church, was a son of Cotton Mather. The group embraces several denominations and diverse political views.

MÆCENAS,[4] you, beneath the myrtle shade,
Read o'er what poets sung, and shepherds play'd.
What felt those poets but you feel the same?
Does not your soul possess the sacred flame?
Their noble strains your equal genius shares
In softer language, and diviner airs.

While *Homer* paints lo! circumfus'd in air,
Celestial Gods in mortal forms appear;
Swift as they move hear each recess rebound,
Heav'n quakes, earth trembles, and the shores resound.
Great Sire of verse, before my mortal eyes,
The lightnings blaze across the vaulted skies,
And, as the thunder shakes the heav'nly plains,
A deep-felt horror thrills through all my veins.
When gentler strains demand thy graceful song,
The length'ning line moves languishing along.
When great *Patroclus* courts *Achilles'* aid,
The grateful tribute of my tears is paid;
Prone on the shore he feels the pangs of love,
And stern *Pelides* tend'rest passions move.

Great *Maro's* strain in heav'nly numbers flows,
The *Nine* inspire, and all the bosom glows.
O could I rival thine and *Virgil's* page,
Or claim the *Muses* with the *Mantuan* Sage;
Soon the same beauties should my mind adorn,
And the same ardors in my soul should burn:
Then should my song in bolder notes arise,
And all my numbers pleasingly surprise;
But here I sit, and mourn a grov'ling mind,
That fain would mount, and ride upon the wind.

Not you, my friend, these plaintive strains become,
Not you, whose bosom is the *Muses* home;
When they from tow'ring *Helicon* retire,

4. The Roman, Gaius Cilnius Mæcenas, was the special friend and patron of Horace and Virgil. Although the 1773 volume of Phillis Wheatley's poems was dedicated to the Countess of Huntingdon, it is more likely that she here is addressing John Wheatley, her master.

They fan in you the bright immortal fire,
But I less happy, cannot raise the song,
The fault'ring music dies upon my tongue.

The happier *Terence** all the choir inspir'd,
His soul replenish'd, and his bosom fir'd;
But say, ye *Muses,* why this partial grace,
To one alone of *Afric's* sable race;
From age to age transmitting thus his name
With the first glory in the rolls of fame?

Thy virtues, great *Mæcenas*! shall be sung
In praise of him, from whom those virtues sprung:
While blooming wreaths around thy temples spread,
I'll snatch a laurel from thine honour'd head,
While you indulgent smile upon the deed.

As long as *Thames* in streams majestic flows,
Or *Naiads* in their oozy beds repose,
While Phœbus reigns above the starry train
While bright *Aurora* purples o'er the main,
So long, great Sir, the muse thy praise shall sing,
So long thy praise shall make *Parnassus* ring:
Then grant, *Mæcenas,* thy paternal rays,
Hear me propitious, and defend my lays.

* He was an African by birth.

ON VIRTUE.

O thou bright jewel in my aim I strive
To comprehend thee. Thine own words declare
Wisdom is higher than a fool can reach.
I cease to wonder, and no more attempt
Thine height t'explore, or fathom thy profound.
But, O my soul, sink not into despair,
Virtue is near thee, and with gentle hand
Would now embrace thee, hovers o'er thine head.
Fain would the heav'n-born soul with her converse,
Then seek, then court her for her promis'd bliss.

Auspicious queen, thine heav'nly pinions spread,
And lead celestial *Chastity* along;
Lo! now her sacred retinue descends,
Array'd in glory from the orbs above.
Attend me, *Virtue,* thro' my youthful years!
O leave me not to the false joys of time!
But guide my steps to endless life and bliss.
Greatness, or *Goodness,* say what I shall call thee,
To give an higher appellation still,
Teach me a better strain, a nobler lay,
O Thou, enthron'd with Cherubs in the realms of
day!

✤✤✤✤✤✤✤

TO THE UNIVERSITY OF CAMBRIDGE, IN NEW-ENGLAND.[5]

WHILE an intrinsic ardor prompts to write,
The muses promise to assist my pen;
'Twas not long since I left my native shore
The land of errors, and *Egyptian* gloom:
Father of mercy, 'twas thy gracious hand
Brought me in safety from those dark abodes.

Students, to you 'tis giv'n to scan the heights
Above, to traverse the ethereal space,
And mark the systems of revolving worlds.
Still more, ye sons of science ye receive
The blissful news by messengers from heav'n,
How *Jesus'* blood for your redemption flows.
See him with hands out-stretcht upon the cross;
Immense compassion in his bosom glows;
He hears revilers, nor resents their scorn:
What matchless mercy in the Son of God!

5. Obviously Harvard University. This poem was written in 1767. According to Samuel Eliot Morrison, *Three Centuries of Harvard 1636-1936* (Cambridge, 1936), 101-32 *passim,* the students at Harvard during this period had a reputation for boisterousness. For the manuscript version of this poem, see Part Two, page 63.

When the whole human race by sin had fall'n,
He deign'd to die that they might rise again,
And share with him in the sublimest skies,
Life without death, and glory without end.

Improve your privileges while they stay,
Ye pupils, and each hour redeem, that bears
Or good or bad report of you to heav'n.
Let sin, that baneful evil to the soul,
By you be shunn'd, nor once remit your guard;
Suppress the deadly serpent in its egg.
Ye blooming plants of human race devine,
An *Ethiop* tells you 'tis your greatest foe;
Its transient sweetness turns to endless pain,
And in immense perdition sinks the soul.

✤✤✤✤✤✤✤

TO THE KING'S MOST EXCELLENT MAJESTY. 1768.

YOUR subjects hope, dread Sire—
The crown upon your brows may flourish long,
And that your arm may in your God be strong!
O may your sceptre num'rous nations sway,
And all with love and readiness obey!

But how shall we the *British* king reward!
Rule thou in peace, our father, and our lord!
Midst the remembrance of thy favours past,
The meanest peasants most admire the last.*
May *George,* belov'd by all the nations round,
Live with heav'ns choicest constant blessings crown'd!
Great God, direct, and guard him from on high,
And from his head let ev'ry evil fly!
And may each clime with equal gladness see
A monarch's smile can set his subjects free!

* The Repeal of the Stamp Act.

ON BEING BROUGHT FROM AFRICA TO AMERICA.

'TWAS mercy brought me from my *Pagan* land,
Taught my benighted soul to understand
That there's a God, that there's a *Saviour* too:
Once I redemption neither sought nor knew.
Some view our sable race with scornful eye,
"Their colour is a diabolic die."
Remember, *Christians, Negroes,* black as *Cain,*
May be refin'd, and join th' angelic train.

****

ON THE DEATH OF THE REV. DR. SEWELL,[6] 1769.

ERE yet the morn its lovely blushes spread,
See *Sewell* number'd with the happy dead.
Hail, holy man, arriv'd th' immortal shore,
Though we shall hear thy warning voice no more.
Come, let us all behold with wishful eyes
The saint ascending to his native skies;
From hence the prophet wing'd his rapt'rous way
To the blest mansions in eternal day.
Then begging for the Spirit of our God,
And panting eager for the same abode,
Come, let us all with the same vigour rise,
And take a prospect of the blissful skies;
While on our minds *Christ's* image is imprest,
And the dear Saviour glows in ev'ry breast.

6. Joseph Sewall (the spelling here is wrong), son of Chief Justice Samuel Sewall and grandfather of a later Chief Justice Samuel Sewall. Elected president of Harvard College in 1724, he declined in order to remain a pastor of Boston's famous Old South Church (Congregational), where he was known for his fervor and devotion and where he became Phillis' pastor (thus her personal reference near the end of this poem). His death in 1769 ended a pastorate there of fifty-six years. (Reference: Justin Winsor, ed., *The Memorial History of Boston,* Vols. II and III, *passim.*) For the manuscript version of this poem, see Part Two, page 64.

Thrice happy saint! to find thy heav'n at last,
What compensation for the evils past!

Great God, incomprehensible, unknown
By sense, we bow at thine exalted throne.
O, while we beg thine excellence to feel,
Thy sacred Spirit to our hearts reveal,
And give us of that mercy to partake,
Which thou hast promis'd for the *Saviour's* sake!

"*Sewell* is dead." Swift-pinion'd *Fame* thus cry'd.
"Is *Sewell* dead," my trembling tongue reply'd,
O what a blessing in his flight deny'd!
How oft for us the holy prophet pray'd!
How oft to us the Word of Life convey'd!
By duty urg'd my mournful verse to close,
I for his tomb this epitaph compose.

"Lo, here a Man, redeem'd by *Jesus'* blood,
"A sinner once, but now a saint with God;
"Behold ye rich, ye poor, ye fools, ye wise,
"Nor let his monument your heart surprise;
" 'Twill tell you what this holy man has done,
"Which gives him brighter lustre than the sun.
"Listen, ye happy, from your seats above.
"I speak sincerely, while I speak and love,
"He sought the paths of piety and truth,
"By these made happy from his early youth;
"In blooming years that grace divine he felt,
"Which rescues sinners from the chains of guilt.
"Mourn him, ye indigent, whom he has fed,
"And henceforth seek, like him, for living bread;
"Ev'n *Christ,* the bread descending from above,
"And ask an int'rest in his saving love.
"Mourn him, ye youth, to whom he oft has told
"God's gracious wonders from the times of old.
"I, too have cause this mighty loss to mourn,
"For he my monitor will not return.
"O when shall we to his blest state arrive?
"When the same graces in our bosoms thrive."

ON THE DEATH OF THE REV. MR. GEORGE WHITEFIELD. 1770.[7]

HAIL, happy saint, on thine immortal throne,
Possest of glory, life, and bliss unknown;
We hear no more the music of thy tongue,
Thy wonted auditories cease to throng.
Thy sermons in unequall'd accents flow'd,
And ev'ry bosom with devotion glow'd;
Thou didst in strains of eloquence refin'd
Inflame the heart, and captivate the mind.
Unhappy we the setting sun deplore,
So glorious once, but ah! it shines no more.

Behold the prophet in his tow'ring flight!
He leaves the earth for heav'n's unmeasur'd height,
And worlds unknown receive him from our sight.
There *Whitefield* wings with rapid course his way,
And sails to *Zion* through vast seas of day.
Thy pray'rs, great saint, and thine incessant cries
Have pierc'd the bosom of thy native skies.
Thou moon hast seen, and all the stars of light,
How he has wrestled with his God by night.
He pray'd that grace in ev'ry heart might dwell,
He long'd to see *America* excel;
He charg'd its youth that ev'ry grace divine
Should with full lustre in their conduct shine;
That Saviour, which his soul did first receive,
The greatest gift that ev'n a God can give,
He freely offer'd to the num'rous throng,
That on his lips with list'ning pleasure hung.

"Take him, ye wretched, for your only good,
"Take him ye starving sinners, for your food;
"Ye thirsty, come to this life-giving stream,
"Ye preachers, take him for your joyful theme;
"Take him my dear *Americans,* he said,

7. Her poem on the death of Whitefield was Phillis' first published work. For earlier published versions and further information concerning this poem, see Part Two, page 66.

"Be your complaints on his kind bosom laid:
"Take him, ye *Africans,* he longs for you,
"*Impartial Saviour* is his title due:
"Wash'd in the fountain of redeeming blood,
"You shall be sons, and kings, and priests to God."

Great *Countess,** we *Americans* revere
Thy name, and mingle in thy grief sincere;
New England deeply feels, the *Orphans* mourn,
Their more than father will no more return.

But, though arrested by the hand of death,
Whitefield no more exerts his lab'ring breath,
Yet let us view him in th' eternal skies,
Let ev'ry heart to this bright vision rise;
While the tomb safe retains its sacred trust,
Till life divine re-animates his dust.

* The Countess of *Huntingdon,* to whom Mr. *Whitefield* was Chaplain.

✤✤✤✤✤✤✤

ON THE DEATH OF A YOUNG LADY OF FIVE YEARS OF AGE.

FROM dark abodes to fair etherial light
Th' enraptur'd innocent has wing'd her flight;
On the kind bosom of eternal love
She finds unknown beatitude above.
This known, ye parents, nor her loss deplore,
She feels the iron hand of pain no more;
The dispensations of unerring grace,
Should turn your sorrows into grateful praise;
Let then no tears for her henceforward flow,
No more distress'd in our dark vale below.

Her morning sun, which rose divinely bright,
Was quickly mantled with the gloom of night;
But hear in heav'n's blest bow'rs your *Nancy* fair,
And learn to imitate her language there.

"Thou, Lord, whom I behold with glory crown'd,
"By what sweet name, and in what tuneful sound
"Wilt thou be prais'd? Seraphic pow'rs are faint
"Infinite love and majesty to paint.
"To thee let all their grateful voices raise,
"And saints and angels join their songs of "praise."

Perfect in bliss she from her heav'nly home
Looks down, and smiling beckons you to come;
Why then, fond parents, why these fruitless groans?
Restrain your tears, and cease your plaintive moans.
Freed from a world of sin, and snares, and pain,
Why would you wish your daughter back again?
No—bow resign'd. Let hope your grief control,
And check the rising tumult of the soul.
Calm in the prosperous, and adverse day,
Adore the God who gives and takes away;
Eye him in all, his holy name revere,
Upright your actions, and your hearts sincere,
Till having sail'd through life's tempestuous sea,
And from its rocks, and boist'rous billows free,
Yourselves, safe landed on the blissful shore,
Shall join your happy babe to part no more.

✤✤✤✤✤✤✤

ON THE DEATH OF A YOUNG GENTLEMAN.

WHO taught thee conflict with the pow'rs of night,
To vanquish Satan in the fields of fight?
Who strung thy feeble arms with might unknown,
How great thy conquest, and how bright thy crown!
War with each princedom, throne, and pow'r is o'er,
The scene is ended to return no more.
O could my muse thy seat on high behold,
How deckt with laurel, how enrich'd with gold!
O could she hear what praise thine harp employs,
How sweet thine anthems, how divine thy joys!

What heav'nly grandeur should exalt her strain!
What holy raptures in her numbers reign!
To sooth the troubles of the mind to peace,
To still the tumult of life's tossing seas,
To ease the anguish of the parents heart,
What shall my sympathizing verse impart?
Where is the balm to heal so deep a wound?
Where shall a sov'reign remedy be found?
Look, gracious Spirit, from thine heav'nly bow'r,
And thy full joys into their bosoms pour;
The raging tempest of their grief control,
And spread the dawn of glory through the soul,
To eye the path the saint departed trod,
And trace him to the bosom of his God.

✤✤✤✤✤✤✤

TO A LADY ON THE DEATH OF HER HUSBAND.[8]

GRIM monarch! see, depriv'd of vital breath,
A young physician in the dust of death:
Dost thou go on incessant to destroy,
Our griefs to double, and lay waste our joy?
Enough thou never yet wast known to say,
Though millions die, the vassals of thy sway:
Nor youth, nor science, nor the ties of love,
Nor ought on earth thy flinty heart can move.
The friend, the spouse from his dire dart to save,
In vain we ask the sovereign of the grave.
Fair mourner, there see thy lov'd *Leonard* laid,
And o'er him spread the deep impervious shade;
Clos'd are his eyes, and heavy fetters keep
His senses bound in never-waking sleep,
Till time shall cease, till many a starry world

8. For the version of this poem printed earlier (in 1771) as "To Mrs. Leonard, on the Death of her Husband," see Part Two, page 71. Mrs. Leonard was the daughter of Thomas Hubbard. (See Phillis' poem to Hubbard on the death of his daughter [p. 46].)

Shall fall from heav'n, in dire confusion hurl'd,
Till nature in her final wreck shall lie,
And her last groan shall rend the azure sky:
Not, not till then his active soul shall claim
His body, a divine immortal frame.

But see the softly-stealing tears apace
Pursue each other down the mourner's face;
But cease thy tears, bid ev'ry sigh depart,
And cast the load of anguish from thine heart:
From the cold shell of his great soul arise,
And look beyond, thou native of the skies;
There fix thy view, where fleeter than the wind
Thy *Leonard* mounts; and leaves the earth behind.
Thyself prepare to pass the vale of night
To join for ever on the hills of light:
To thine embrace his joyful spirit moves
To thee, the partner of his earthly loves;
He welcomes thee to pleasures more refin'd,
And better suited to th' immortal mind.

✤✤✤✤✤✤✤

GOLIATH OF GATH.
I Sam. Chap. XVII

YE martial pow'rs, and all ye tuneful nine,
Inspire my song, and aid my high design.
The dreadful scenes and toils of war I write,
The ardent warriors, and the fields of fight:
You best remember, and you best can sing
The acts of heroes to the vocal string:
Resume the lays with which your sacred lyre,
Did then the poet and the sage inspire.

Now front to front the armies were display'd,
Here *Israel* rang'd, and there the foes array'd;
The hosts on two opposing mountains stood,
Thick as the foliage of the waving wood;

Between them an extensive valley lay,
O'er which the gleaming armour pour'd the day,
When from the camp of the *Philistine* foes,
Dreadful to view, a mighty warrior rose;
In the dire deeds of bleeding battle skill'd,
The monster stalks the terror of the field.
From *Gath* he sprung, *Goliath* was his name,
Of fierce deportment, and gigantic frame:
A brazen helmet on his head was plac'd,
A coat of mail his form terrific grac'd,
The greaves his legs, the targe his shoulders prest:
Dreadful in arms high-tow'ring o'er the rest
A spear he proudly wav'd, whose iron head,
Strange to relate, six hundred shekels weigh'd;
He strode along, and shook the ample field,
While *Phœbus* blaz'd refulgent on his shield:
Through *Jacob's* race a chilling horror ran,
When thus the huge, enormous chief began:

"Say, what the cause that in this proud array
"You set your battle in the face of day?
"One hero find in all your vaunting train,
"Then see who loses, and who wins the plain;
"For he who wins, in triumph may demand
"Perpetual service from the vanquish'd land:
"Your armies I defy, your force despise,
"By far inferior in *Philistia's* eyes:
"Produce a man, and let us try the fight,
"Decide the contest, and the victor's right."

Thus challeng'd he: all *Israel* stood amaz'd,
And ev'ry chief in consternation gaz'd;
But *Jesse's* son in youthful bloom appears,
And warlike courage far beyond his years:
He left the folds, he left the flow'ry meads,
And soft recesses of the sylvan shades.
Now *Israel's* monarch, and his troops arise,
With peals of shouts ascending to the skies;
In *Elah's* vale the scene of combat lies.

When the fair morning blush'd with orient red,
What *David's* sire enjoin'd the son obey'd,
And swift of foot toward the trench he came,
Where glow'd each bosom with the martial flame.
He leaves his carriage to another's care,
And runs to greet his brethren of the war.
While yet they spake the giant-chief arose,
Repeats the challenge, and insults his foes:
Struck with the sound, and trembling at the view,
Affrighted *Israel* from its post withdrew.
"Observe ye this tremendous foe, they cry'd,
"Who in proud vaunts our armies hath defy'd:
"Whoever lays him prostrate on the plain,
"Freedom in *Israel* for his house shall gain;
"And on him wealth unknown the king will pour,
"And give his royal daughter for his dow'r."

Then *Jesse's* youngest hope: "My brethren say,"
"What shall be done for him who takes away
"Reproach from *Jacob,* who destroys the chief,
"And puts a period to his country's grief.
"He vaunts the honours of his arms abroad,
"And scorns the armies of the living God."

Thus spoke the youth, th' attentive people ey'd
The wond'rous hero, and again reply'd:
"Such the rewards our monarch will bestow,
"On him who conquers, and destroys his foe."

Eliab heard, and kindled into ire
To hear his shepherd brother thus inquire,
And thus begun: "What errand brought thee? say
"Who keeps thy flock? or does it go astray?
"I know the base ambition of thine heart,
"But back in safety from the field depart."

Eliab thus to *Jesse's* youngest heir,
Express'd his wrath in accents most severe.
When to his brother mildly he reply'd,
"What have I done? or what the cause to chide?"

The words were told before the king, who sent
For the young hero to his royal tent:
Before the monarch dauntless he began,
"For this *Philistine* fail no heart of man:
"I'll take the vale, and with the giant fight:
"I dread not all his boasts, nor all his might."
When thus the king: "Dar'st thou a stripling go,
"And venture combat with so great a foe?
"Who all his days has been inur'd to fight,
"And made its deeds his study and delight:
"Battles and bloodshed brought the monster forth,
"And clouds and whirlwinds usher'd in his birth."
When *David* thus: "I kept the fleecy care,
"And out there rush'd a lion and a bear;
"A tender lamb the hungry lion took,
"And with no other weapon than my crook
"Bold I pursu'd, and chas'd him o'er the field,
"The prey deliver'd, and the felon kill'd:
"As thus the lion and the bear I slew,
"So shall *Goliath* fall, and all his crew:
"The God, who sav'd me from these beasts of prey,
"By me this monster in the dust shall lay."
So *David* spoke. The wond'ring king reply'd;
"Go thou with heav'n and victory on thy side:
"This coat of mail, this sword gird on," he said,
And plac'd a mighty helmet on his head:
The coat, the sword, the helm he laid aside,
Nor chose to venture with those arms untry'd,
Then took his staff, and to the neighb'ring brook
Instant he ran, and thence five pebbles took.
Mean time descended to *Philistia's* son
A radiant cherub, and he thus begun:
"*Goliath,* well thou know'st thou hast defy'd
"Yon Hebrew armies, and their God deny'd:
"Rebellious wretch! audacious worm! forbear,
"Nor tempt the vengeance of their God too far:
"Them, who with his omnipotence contend,
"No eye shall pity, and no arm defend:

"Proud as thou art, in short liv'd glory great,
"I come to tell thee thine approaching fate.
"Regard my words. The judge of all the gods,
"Beneath whose steps the tow'ring mountain nods,
"Will give thine armies to the savage brood,
"That cut the liquid air, or range the wood.
"Thee too a well-aim'd pebble shall destroy,
"And thou shalt perish by a beardless boy:
"Such is the mandate from the realms above,
"And should I try the vengeance to remove,
"Myself a rebel to my king would prove.
"*Goliath* say, shall grace to him be shown,
"Who dares heav'ns monarch, and insults his throne?"

"Your words are lost on me," the giant cries,
While fear and wrath contended in his eyes,
When thus the messenger from heav'n replies:
"Provoke no more *Jehovah's* awful hand
"To hurl its vengeance on thy guilty land:
"He grasps the thunder, and, he wings the storm,
"Servants their sov'reign's orders to perform."

The angel spoke, and turn'd his eyes away,
Adding new radiance to the rising day.

Now *David* comes: the fatal stones demand
His left, the staff engag'd his better hand:
The giant mov'd, and from his tow'ring height
Survey'd the stripling, and disdain'd the sight,
And thus began: "Am I a dog with thee?
"Bring'st thou no armour, but a staff to me?
"The gods on thee their vollied curses pour,
"And beasts and birds of prey thy flesh devour."

David undaunted thus, "Thy spear and shield
"Shall no protection to thy body yield:
"*Jehovah's* name ------ no other arms I bear,
"I ask no other in this glorious war.
"To-day the Lord of Hosts to me will give
"Vict'ry, to-day thy doom thou shalt receive;

"The fate you threaten shall your own become,
"And beasts shall be your animated tomb,
"That all the earth's inhabitants may know
"That there's a God, who governs all below:
"This great assembly too shall witness stand,
"That needs nor sword, nor spear, th' Almighty's hand:
"The battle his, the conquest he bestows,
"And to our pow'r consigns our hated foes."

Thus *David* spoke; *Goliath* heard and came
To meet the hero in the field of fame.
Ah! fatal meeting to thy troops and thee,
But thou wast deaf to the divine decree;
Young *David* meets thee, meets thee not in vain;
'Tis thine to perish on th' ensanguin'd plain.

And now the youth the forceful pebble flung,
Philistia trembled as it whizz'd along:
In his dread forehead, where the helmet ends,
Just o'er the brows the well-aim'd stone descends,
It pierc'd the skull, and shatter'd all the brain,
Prone on his face he tumbled to the plain:
Goliath's fall no smaller terror yields
Than riving thunders in aerial fields:
The soul still ling'red in its lov'd abode,
Till conq'ring *David* o'er the giant strode:
Goliath's sword then laid its master dead,
And from the body hew'd the ghastly head;
The blood in gushing torrents drench'd the plains,
The soul found passage through the spouting veins.

And now aloud th' illustrious victor said,
"Where are your boastings now your champion's dead?"
Scarce had he spoke, when the *Philistines* fled:
But fled in vain; the conqu'ror swift pursu'd:
What scenes of slaughter! and what seas of blood!
There *Saul* thy thousands grasp'd th' impurpled sand
In pangs of death the conquest of thine hand;
And *David* there were thy ten thousands laid:
Thus *Israel's* damsels musically play'd.

Near *Gath* and *Ekron* many an hero lay,
Breath'd out their souls, and curs'd the light of day:
Their fury, quench'd by death, no longer burns,
And *David* with *Goliath's* head returns,
To *Salem* brought, but in his tent he plac'd
The load of armour which the giant grac'd.
His monarch saw him coming from the war,
And thus demanded of the son of *Ner.*
"Say, who is this amazing youth?" he cry'd,
When thus the leader of the host reply'd;
"As lives thy soul I know not whence he sprung,
"So great in prowess though in years so young:"
"Inquire whose son is he," the sov'reign said,
"Before whose conq'ring arm *Philistia* fled."
Before the king behold the stripling stand,
Goliath's head depending from his hand:
To him the king: "Say of what martial line
"Art thou, young hero, and what sire was thine?"
He humbly thus; "the son of *Jesse* I:
"I came the glories of the field to try.
"Small is my tribe, but valiant in the fight;
"Small is my city, but thy royal right."
"Then take the promis'd gifts," the monarch cry'd,
Conferring riches and the royal bride:
"Knit to my soul for ever thou remain
"With me, nor quit my regal roof again."

✤✤✤✤✤✤✤

THOUGHTS ON THE WORKS OF PROVIDENCE.[9]

ARISE, my soul, on wings enraptur'd, rise
To praise the monarch of the earth and skies,

9. This poem was later published by E. Gay in Halifax in 1805 as an eight-page pamphlet. The title page of the pamphlet read *A Beautiful Poem on Providence,* but at the head of the poem was the title given here. (The Library of Congress has a copy, in fragile condition.) The poem was well chosen for a separate printing. It has some good lines and suggests an influence by Milton.

Whose goodness and benificence appear
As round its centre moves the rolling year,
Or when the morning glows with rosy charms,
Or the sun slumbers in the ocean's arms:
Of light divine be a rich portion lent
To guide my soul, and favour my intent.
Celestial muse, my arduous flight sustain,
And raise my mind to a seraphic strain!

Ador'd for ever be the God unseen,
Which round the sun revolves this vast machine,
Though to his eye its mass a point appears:
Ador'd the God that whirls surrounding spheres,
Which first ordain'd that mighty *Sol* should reign
The peerless monarch of th' ethereal train:
Of miles twice forty millions is his height,
And yet his radiance dazzles mortal sight
So far beneath—from him th' extended earth
Vigour derives, and ev'ry flow'ry birth:
Vast through her orb she moves with easy grace
Around her *Phœbus* in unbounded space;
True to her course th' impetuous storm derides,
Triumphant o'er the winds, and surging tides.

Almighty, in these wond'rous works of thine,
What *Pow'r,* what *Wisdom,* and what *Goodness* shine!
And are thy wonders, Lord, by men explor'd,
And yet creating glory unador'd!

Creation smiles in various beauty gay,
While day to night, and night succeeds to day:
That *Wisdom,* which attends *Jehovah's* ways,
Shines most conspicuous in the solar rays:
Without them, destitute of heat and light,
This world would be the reign of endless night:
In their excess how would our race complain,
Abhorring life! how hate its length'ned chain!
From air adust what num'rous ills would rise?
What dire contagion taint the burning skies?

What pestilential vapours, fraught with death,
Would rise, and overspread the lands beneath?

Hail, smiling morn, that from the orient main
Ascending dost adorn the heav'nly plain!
So rich, so various are thy beauteous dies,
That spread through all the circuit of the skies,
That, full of thee, my soul in rapture soars,
And thy great God, the cause of all adores.

O'er beings infinite his love extends,
His *Wisdom* rules them, and his *Pow'r* defends.
When tasks diurnal tire the human frame,
The spirits faint, and dim the vital flame,
Then too that ever active bounty shines,
Which not infinity of space confines.
The sable veil, that *Night* in silence draws,
Conceals effects, but shews th' *Almighty Cause*;
Night seals in sleep the wide creation fair,
And all is peaceful but the brow of care.
Again, gay *Phœbus,* as the day before,
Wakes ev'ry eye, but what shall wake no more;
Again the face of nature is renew'd,
Which still appears harmonious, fair, and good.
May grateful strains salute the smiling morn,
Before its beams the eastern hills adorn!

Shall day to day, and night to night conspire
To show the goodness of the Almighty Sire?
This mental voice shall man regardless hear,
And never, never raise the filial pray'r?
To-day, O hearken, nor your folly mourn
For time mispent, that never will return.

But see the sons of vegetation rise,
And spread their leafy banners to the skies.
All-wise Almighty providence we trace
In trees, and plants, and all the flow'ry race;
As clear as in the nobler frame of man,
All lovely copies of the Maker's plan.

The pow'r the same that forms a ray of light,
That call'd creation from eternal night.
"Let there be light," he said: from his profound
Old *Chaos* heard, and trembled at the sound:
Swift as the word, inspir'd by pow'r divine,
Behold the light around its maker shine,
The first fair product of th' omnific God,
And now through all his works diffus'd abroad.

As reason's pow'rs by day our God disclose,
So we may trace him in the night's repose:
Say what is sleep? and dreams how passing strange!
When action ceases, and ideas range
Licentious and unbounded o'er the plains,
Where *Fancy's* queen in giddy triumph reigns.
Hear in soft strains the dreaming lover sigh
To a kind fair, or rave in jealousy;
On pleasure now, and now on vengeance bent,
The lab'ring passions struggle for a vent.
What pow'r, O man! thy *reason* then restores,
So long suspended in nocturnal hours?
What secret hand returns the mental train,
And gives improv'd thine active pow'rs again?
From thee, O man, what gratitude should rise!
And, when from balmy sleep thou op'st thine eyes,
Let thy first thoughts be praises to the skies.
How merciful our God who thus imparts
O'erflowing tides of joy to human hearts,
When wants and woes might be our righteous lot,
Our God forgetting, by our God forgot!

Among the mental pow'rs a question rose,
"What most the image of th' Eternal shows?"
When thus to *Reason* (so let *Fancy* rove)
Her great companion spoke, immortal *Love*.

"Say, mighty pow'r, how long shall strife prevail,
"And with its murmurs load the whisp'ring gale?
"Refer the cause to *Recollection's* shrine,
"Who loud proclaims my origin divine,

"The cause whence heav'n and earth began to be,
"And is not man immortaliz'd by me?
"*Reason* let this most causeless strife subside."
Thus *Love* pronounc'd, and *Reason* thus reply'd.

"Thy birth, celestial queen! 'tis mine to own,
"In thee resplendent is the Godhead shown;
"Thy words persuade, my soul enraptur'd feels
"Resistless beauty which thy smile reveals."
Ardent she spoke, and, kindling at her charms,
She clasp'd the blooming goddess in her arms.

Infinite *Love* wher'er we turn our eyes
Appears: this ev'ry creature's wants supplies;
This most is heard in *Nature's* constant voice,
This makes the morn, and this the eve rejoice;
This bids the fost'ring rains and dews descend
To nourish all, to serve one gen'ral end,
The good of man: yet man ungrateful pays
But little homage, and but little praise.
To him, whose works array'd with mercy shine,
What songs should rise, how constant, how divine!

✤✤✤✤✤✤✤

TO A LADY ON THE DEATH OF THREE RELATIONS.

WE trace the pow'r of Death from tomb to tomb,
And his are all the ages yet to come.
'Tis his to call the planets from on high,
To blacken *Phœbus,* and dissolve the sky;
His too, when all in his dark realms are hurl'd,
From its firm base to shake the solid world;
His fatal sceptre rules the spacious whole,
And trembling nature rocks from pole to pole.

Awful he moves, and wide his wings are spread:
Behold thy brother number'd with the dead!
From bondage freed, the exulting spirit flies

Beyond *Olympus,* and these starry skies.
Lost in our woe for thee, blest shade, we mourn
In vain; to earth thou never must return.
Thy sisters too, fair mourner, feel the dart
Of Death, and with fresh torture rend thine heart.
Weep not for them, who wish thine happy mind
To rise with them, and leave the world behind.

As a young plant by hurricanes up torn,
So near its parent lies the newly born—
But 'midst the bright ethereal train behold
It shines superior on a throne of gold:
Then, mourner, cease; let hope thy tears restrain,
Smile on the tomb, and sooth the raging pain.
On yon blest regions fix thy longing view,
Mindless of sublunary scenes below;
Ascend the sacred mount, in thought arise,
And seek substantial and immortal joys;
Where hope receives, where faith to vision springs,
And raptur'd seraphs tune th' immortal strings
To strains extatic. Thou the chorus join,
And to thy father tune the praise divine.

✤✤✤✤✤✤✤

TO A CLERGYMAN ON THE DEATH OF HIS LADY.[10]

WHERE contemplation finds her sacred spring,
Where heav'nly music makes the arches ring,
Where virtue reigns unsully'd and divine,
Where wisdom thron'd, and all the graces shine,
There sits thy spouse amidst the radiant throng,
While praise eternal warbles from her tongue;
There choirs angelic shout her welcome round,
With perfect bliss, and peerless glory crown'd.

10. For the version of this poem published earlier (in 1772) as "To the Rev. Mr. Pitkin, on the Death of his Lady," see Part Two, page 76.

While thy dear mate, to flesh no more confin'd,
Exults a blest, an heav'n-ascended mind,
Say in thy breast shall floods of sorrow rise?
Say shall its torrents overwhelm thine eyes?
Amid the seats of heav'n a place is free,
And angels open their bright ranks for thee;
For thee they wait, and with expectant eye
Thy spouse leans downward from th' empyreal sky:
"O come away, her longing spirit cries,
"And share with me the raptures of the skies.
"Our bliss divine to mortals is unknown;
"Immortal life and glory are our own.
"There too may the dear pledges of our love
"Arrive, and taste with us the joys above;
"Attune the harp to more than mortal lays,
"And join with us the tribute of their praise
"To him, who dy'd stern justice to atone,
"And make eternal glory all our own.
"He in his death slew ours, and, as he rose,
"He crush'd the dire dominion of our foes;
"Vain were their hopes to put the God to flight,
"Chain us to hell, and bar the gates of light."

She spoke, and turn'd from mortal scenes her eyes,
Which beam'd celestial radiance o'er the skies.

Then thou, dear man, no more with grief retire,
Let grief no longer damp devotiŏn's fire,
But rise sublime, to equal bliss aspire.
Thy sighs no more be wafted by the wind,
No more complain, but be to heav'n resign'd.
'Twas thine t' unfold the oracles divine,
To sooth our woes the task was also thine;
Now sorrow is incumbent on thy heart,
Permit the muse a cordial to impart;
Who can to thee their tend'rest aid refuse?
To dry thy tears how longs the heav'nly muse!

AN HYMN TO THE MORNING.

ATTEND my lays, ye ever honour'd nine,
Assist my labours, and my strains refine;
In smoothest numbers pour the notes along,
For bright *Aurora* now demands my song.

Aurora hail, and all the thousand dies,
Which deck thy progress through the vaulted skies:
The morn awakes, and wide extends her rays,
On ev'ry leaf the gentle zephyr plays;
Harmonious lays the feather'd race resume,
Dart the bright eye, and shake the painted plume.

Ye shady groves, your verdant gloom display
To shield your poet from the burning day:
Calliope awake the sacred lyre,
While thy fair sisters fan the pleasing fire:
The bow'rs, the gales, the variegated skies
In all their pleasures in my bosom rise.

See in the east th' illustrious king of day!
His rising radiance drives the shades away—
But Oh! I feel his fervid beams too strong,
And scarce begun, concludes th' abortive song.

✤✤✤✤✤✤✤

AN HYMN TO THE EVENING.

SOON as the sun forsook the eastern main
The pealing thunder shook the heav'nly plain;
Majestic grandeur! From the zephyr's wing,
Exhales the incense of the blooming spring.
Soft purl the streams, the birds renew their notes,
And through the air their mingled music floats.

Through all the heav'ns what beauteous dies are spread!
But the west glories in the deepest red:
So may our breasts with ev'ry virtue glow,
The living temples of our God below!

Fill'd with the praise of him who gives the light;
And draws the sable curtains of the night,
Let placid slumbers sooth each weary mind,
At morn to wake more heav'nly, more refin'd;
So shall the labours of the day begin
More pure, more guarded from the snares of sin.

Night's leaden sceptre seals my drousy eyes,
Then cease, my song, till fair *Aurora* rise.

✤✤✤✤✤✤✤

ISAIAH LXIII. 1–8.

SAY, heav'nly muse, what king, or mighty God,
That moves sublime from *Idumea's* road?
In *Bozrah's* dies, with martial glories join'd,
His purple vesture waves upon the wind.
Why thus enrob'd delights he to appear
In the dread image of the *Pow'r* of war?

Compres'd in wrath the swelling wine-press groan'd,
It bled, and pour'd the gushing purple round.

"Mine was the act," th' Almighty Saviour said,
And shook the dazzling glories of his head,
"When all forsook I trod the press alone,
"And conquer'd by omnipotence my own;
"For man's release sustain'd the pond'rous load,
"For man the wrath of an immortal God:
"To execute th' Eternal's dread command
"My soul I sacrific'd with willing hand;
"Sinless I stood before the avenging frown,
"Atoning thus for vices not my own."

His eye the ample field of battle round
Survey'd, but no created succours found;
His own omnipotence sustain'd the fight,
His vengeance sunk the haughty foes in night;
Beneath his feet the prostrate troops were spread,
And round him lay the dying, and the dead.

Great God, what light'ning flashes from thine eyes?
What pow'r withstands if thou indignant rise?

Against thy *Zion* though her foes may rage,
And all their cunning, all their strength engage,
Yet she serenely on thy bosom lies,
Smiles at their arts, and all their force defies.

✤✤✤✤✤✤✤

ON RECOLLECTION.[11]

MNEME begin. Inspire, ye sacred nine,
Your vent'rous *Afric* in her great design.
Mneme, immortal pow'r, I trace thy spring:
Assist my strains, while I thy glories sing:
The acts of long departed years, by thee
Recover'd, in due order rang'd we see:
Thy pow'r the long-forgotten calls from night,
That sweetly plays before the *fancy's* sight.

Mneme in our nocturnal visions pours
The ample treasure of her secret stores;
Swift from above she wings her silent flight
Through *Phœbe's* realms, fair regent of the night;
And, in her pomp of images display'd,
To the high-raptur'd poet gives her aid,
Through the unbounded regions of the mind,
Diffusing light celestial and refin'd.
The heav'nly *phantom* paints the actions done
By ev'ry tribe beneath the rolling sun.

Mneme, enthron'd within the human breast,
Has vice condemn'd, and ev'ry virtue blest.
How sweet the sound when we her plaudit hear?
Sweeter than music to the ravish'd ear,
Sweeter than *Maro's* entertaining strains
Resounding through the groves, and hills, and plains.

11. For the earlier published version of this poem, see Part Two, page 73.

But how is *Mneme* dreaded by the race,
Who scorn her warnings and despise her grace?
By her unveil'd each horrid crime appears,
Her awful hand a cup of wormwood bears.
Days, years mispent, O what a hell of woe!
Hers the worst tortures that our souls can know.

Now eighteen years their destin'd course have run,
In fast succession round the central sun.
How did the follies of that period pass
Unnotic'd, but behold them writ in brass!
In Recollection see them fresh return,
And sure 'tis mine to be asham'd, and mourn.

O *Virtue,* smiling in immortal green,
Do thou exert thy pow'r, and change the scene;
Be thine employ to guide my future days,
And mine to pay the tribute of my praise.

Of *Recollection* such the pow'r enthron'd
In ev'ry breast, and thus her pow'r is own'd.
The wretch, who dar'd the vengeance of the skies,
At last awakes in horror and surprise,
By her alarm'd, he sees impending fate,
He howls in anguish, and repents too late.
But O! what peace, what joys are hers t' impart
To ev'ry holy, ev'ry upright heart!
Thrice blest the man, who, in her sacred shrine,
Feels himself shelter'd from the wrath divine!

✤✤✤✤✤✤✤

ON IMAGINATION.

THY various works, imperial queen, we see,
How bright their forms! how deck'd with pomp by thee!
Thy wond'rous acts in beauteous order stand,
And all attest how potent is thine hand.

From *Helicon's* refulgent heights attend,
Ye sacred choir, and my attempts befriend:

To tell her glories with a faithful tongue,
Ye blooming graces, triumph in my song.

Now here, now there, the roving *Fancy* flies,
Till some lov'd object strikes her wand'ring eyes,
Whose silken fetters all the senses bind,
And soft captivity involves the mind.

Imagination! who can sing thy force?
Or who describe the swiftness of thy course?
Soaring through air to find the bright abode,
Th' empyreal palace of the thund'ring God,
We on thy pinions can surpass the wind,
And leave the rolling universe behind:
From star to star the mental optics rove,
Measure the skies, and range the realms above.
There in one view we grasp the mighty whole,
Or with new worlds amaze th' unbounded soul.

Though *Winter* frowns to *Fancy's* raptur'd eyes
The fields may flourish, and gay scenes arise;
The frozen deeps may break their iron bands,
And bid their waters murmur o'er the sands.
Fair *Flora* may resume her fragrant reign,
And with her flow'ry riches deck the plain;
Sylvanus may diffuse his honours round,
And all the forest may with leaves be crown'd:
Show'rs may descend, and dews their gems disclose,
And nectar sparkle on the blooming rose.

Such is thy pow'r, nor are thine orders vain,
O thou the leader of the mental train:
In full perfection all thy works are wrought,
And thine the sceptre o'er the realms of thought.
Before thy throne the subject-passions bow,
Of subject-passions sov'reign ruler Thou,
At thy command joy rushes on the heart,
And through the glowing veins the spirits dart.

Fancy might now her silken pinions try
To rise from earth, and sweep th' expanse on high;

From *Tithon's* bed now might *Aurora* rise,
Her cheeks all glowing with celestial dies,
While a pure stream of light o'erflows the skies.
The monarch of the day I might behold,
And all the mountains tipt with radiant gold,
But I reluctant leave the pleasing views,
Which *Fancy* dresses to delight the *Muse*;
Winter austere forbids me to aspire,
And northern tempests damp the rising fire;
They chill the tides of *Fancy's* flowing sea,
Cease then, my song, cease the unequal lay.

✣✣✣✣✣✣✣

A FUNERAL POEM ON THE DEATH OF C. E. AN INFANT OF TWELVE MONTHS.

THROUGH airy roads he wings his instant flight
To purer regions of celestial light;
Enlarg'd he sees unnumber'd systems roll,
Beneath him sees the universal whole,
Planets on planets run their destin'd round,
And circling wonders fill the vast profound.
Th' ethereal now, and now th' empyreal skies
With growing splendors strike his wond'ring eyes:
The angels view him with delight unknown,
Press his soft hand, and seat him on his throne;
Then smiling thus. "To this divine abode,
"The seat of saints, of seraphs, and of God,
"Thrice welcome thou." The raptur'd babe replies,
"Thanks to my God, who snatch'd me to the skies,
"E'er vice triumphant had possess'd my heart,
"E'er yet the tempter had beguil'd my heart,
"E'er yet on sin's base actions I was bent,
"E'er yet I knew temptation's dire intent;
"E'er yet the lash for horrid crimes I felt,
"E'er vanity had led my way to guilt,
"But, soon arriv'd at my celestial goal,

"Full glories rush on my expanding soul."
Joyful he spoke: exulting cherubs round
Clapt their glad wings, the heav'nly vaults resound.

Say, parents, why this unavailing moan?
Why heave your pensive bosoms with the groan?
To *Charles,* the happy subject of my song,
A brighter world, and nobler strains belong.
Say would you tear him from the realms above
By thoughtless wishes, and prepost'rous love?
Doth his felicity increase your pain?
Or could you welcome to this world again
The heir of bliss? with a superior air
Methinks he answers with a smile severe,
"Thrones and dominions cannot tempt me there."
But still you cry, "Can we the sigh forbear,
"And still and still must we not pour the tear?
"Our only hope, more dear than vital breath,
"Twelve moons revolv'd, becomes the prey of death;
"Delightful infant, nightly visions give
"Thee to our arms, and we with joy receive,
"We fain would clasp the *Phantom* to our breast,
"The *Phantom* flies, and leaves the soul unblest."

To yon bright regions let your faith ascend,
Prepare to join your dearest infant friend
In pleasures without measure, without end.

TO CAPTAIN H——D, OF THE 65TH REGIMENT.

SAY, muse divine, can hostile scenes delight
The warrior's bosom in the fields of fight?
Lo! here the christian and the hero join
With mutual grace to form the man divine.
In H——d see with pleasure and surprise,
Where *valour* kindles, and where *virtue* lies:

Go, hero brave, still grace the post of fame,
And add new glories to thine honour'd name,
Still to the field, and still to virtue true:
Britannia glories in no son like you.

✤✤✤✤✤✤✤

TO THE RIGHT HONOURABLE WILLIAM, EARL OF DARTMOUTH, HIS MAJESTY'S PRINCIPAL SECRETARY OF STATE FOR NORTH-AMERICA, &C.[12]

HAIL, happy day, when, smiling like the morn,
Fair *Freedom* rose *New-England* to adorn:
The northern clime beneath her genial ray,
Dartmouth, congratulates thy blissful sway:
Elate with hope her race no longer mourns,
Each soul expands, each grateful bosom burns,
While in thine hand with pleasure we behold
The silken reins, and *Freedom's* charms unfold.
Long lost to realms beneath the northern skies

12. William Legge, Second Earl of Dartmouth, (1731-1801), who in August, 1772, became Secretary of State for the Colonies and President of the Board of Trade and Foreign Plantations in Lord North's administration, which appointment he retained until November, 1775. Presumably, this poem was written soon after word of his appointment was received in Boston. It was sent to Dartmouth with a letter dated October 10, 1772 (see the letter in the appendix to this volume [p. 110]). Phillis' hopes proved to be false ones, as he proved to be a minister not in sympathy with the events which occurred in New England in the following months.

Dartmouth was a friend of the Countess of Huntingdon (see the dedication to the 1773 volume) and to the methodist movement. He was also an acquaintance of Samson Occom, who was involved in the founding of Dartmouth College, which was named for this Earl. (In Harold Blodgett, *Samson Occom* [Hanover, N.H., 1935], pp. 119, 148, are letters of March 5, 1771, and September 21, 1773, from Occom to Mrs. Wheatley in which he sends greetings to Phillis. Mrs. Wheatley was apparently helping Occom in some project. The Archives Department of the Dartmouth College Library also has a letter of December 31, 1768 [ms. 765681.2] from Mrs. Wheatley in Boston to Occom, apparently in England, in which she says, "Please to give my love to the Reverend

She shines supreme, while hated *faction* dies:
Soon as appear'd the *Goddess* long desir'd,
Sick at the view, she lanquish'd and expir'd;
Thus from the splendors of the morning light
The owl in sadness seeks the caves of night.

No more, *America,* in mournful strain
Of wrongs, and grievance unredress'd complain,
No longer shalt thou dread the iron chain,
Which wanton *Tyranny* with lawless hand
Had made, and with it meant t' enslave the land.

Should you, my lord, while you peruse my song,
Wonder from whence my love of *Freedom* sprung,
Whence flow these wishes for the common good,
By feeling hearts alone best understood,
I, young in life, by seeming cruel fate
Was snatch'd from *Afric's* fancy'd happy seat:
What pangs excruciating must molest,
What sorrows labour in my parent's breast?
Steel'd was that soul and by no misery mov'd
That from a father seiz'd his babe belov'd:
Such, such my case. And can I then but pray
Others may never feel tyrannic sway?

For favours past, great Sir, our thanks are due,
And thee we ask thy favours to renew,
Since in thy pow'r, as in thy will before,
To sooth the griefs, which thou did'st once deplore.

Mr. Whitefield & beg his Prayers for my self and family.") It is certain that Dartmouth, Occom, Whitefield, and the Countess of Huntingdon were mutual acquaintances, and this fact may have paved the way for Phillis' interest in the three from England. It is quite likely that Mrs. Wheatley at least heard Whitefield preach, and Phillis may have also. Mrs. Wheatley apparently made a trip to England in October of 1772 (see the "Ode to Neptune," page 35), and she may have met Dartmouth and the Countess then. It is certain that Phillis met them both during her visit to England in 1773, and she probably was accompanied by Nathaniel Wheatley in these encounters. Dartmouth gave her a copy of a translation of *Don Quixote*. (See the Introduction and A Note on Text to this volume and the notes to Phillis' poems on Whitefield's death [pp. 9 and 66].)

May heav'nly grace the sacred sanction give
To all thy works, and thou for ever live
Not only on the wings of fleeting *Fame,*
Though praise immortal crowns the patriot's name,
But to conduct to heav'ns refulgent fane,
May fiery coursers sweep th' ethereal plain,
And bear thee upwards to that blest abode,
Where, like the prophet, thou shalt find thy God.

✠✠✠✠✠✠✠

ODE TO NEPTUNE.

On Mrs. W—'s[13] *Voyage to England.*

I.

WHILE raging tempests shake the shore,
While *Æ'lus'* thunders round us roar,
And sweep impetuous o'er the plain
Be still, O tyrant of the main;
Nor let thy brow contracted frowns betray,
While my *Susannah* skims the wat'ry way.

II.

The *Pow'r* propitious hears the lay,
The blue-ey'd daughters of the sea
With sweeter cadence glide along,
And *Thames* responsive joins the song.
Pleas'd with their notes *Sol* sheds benign his ray,
And double radiance decks the face by day.

III.

To court thee to *Britannia's* arms
  Serene the climes and mild the sky,
Her region boasts unnumber'd charms,
  Thy welcome smiles in ev'ry eye.
Thy promise, *Neptune* keep, record my pray'r,
Nor give my wishes to the empty air.

Boston, October 10 1772.

13. Undoubtedly Mrs. Susannah Wheatley, Phillis' mistress, of whom she was quite fond.

TO A LADY ON HER COMING TO NORTH-AMERICA WITH HER SON, FOR THE RECOVERY OF HER HEALTH.

INDULGENT muse! my grov'ling mind inspire,
And fill my bosom with celestial fire.

See from *Jamaica's* fervid shore she moves,
Like the fair mother of the blooming loves,
When from above the *Goddess* with her hand
Fans the soft breeze, and lights upon the land;
Thus she on *Neptune's* wat'ry realm reclin'd
Appear'd, and thus invites the ling'ring wind.

"Arise, ye winds, *America* explore,
"Waft me, ye gales, from this malignant shore;
"The *Northern* milder climes I long to greet,
"There hope that health will my arrival meet."
Soon as she spoke in my ideal view
The winds assented, and the vessel flew.

Madam, your spouse bereft of wife and son,
In the grove's dark recesses pours his moan;
Each branch, wide-spreading to the ambient sky,
Forgets its verdure, and submits to die.

From thence I turn, and leave the sultry plain,
And swift pursue thy passage o'er the main:
The ship arrives before the fav'ring wind,
And makes the *Philadelphian* port assign'd,
Thence I attend you to *Bostonia's* arms,
Where gen'rous friendship ev'ry bosom warms:
Thrice welcome here! may health revive again,
Bloom on thy cheek, and bound in ev'ry vein!
Then back return to gladden ev'ry heart,
And give your spouse his soul's far dearer part,
Receiv'd again with what a sweet surprise,
The tear in transport starting from his eyes!
While his attendant son with blooming grace

Springs to his father's ever dear embrace.
With shouts of joy *Jamaica's* rocks resound,
With shouts of joy the country rings around.

✦✦✦✦✦✦✦

TO A LADY ON HER REMARKABLE PRESERVATION IN AN HURRICANE IN NORTH-CAROLINA.

THOUGH thou did'st hear the tempest from afar,
And felt'st the horrors of the wat'ry war,
To me unknown, yet on this peaceful shore
Methinks I hear the storm tumultuous roar,
And how stern *Boreas* with impetuous hand
Compell'd the *Nereids* to usurp the land.
Reluctant rose the daughters of the main,
And slow ascending glided o'er the plain,
Till *Æolus* in his rapid chariot drove
In gloomy grandeur from the vault above:
Furious he comes. His winged sons obey
Their frantic sire, and madden all the sea.
The billows rave, the wind's fierce tyrant roars,
And with his thund'ring terrors shakes the shores:
Broken by waves the vessel's frame is rent,
And strows with planks the wat'ry element.

But thee, *Maria,* a kind *Nereid's* shield
Preserv'd from sinking, and thy form upheld:
And sure some heav'nly oracle design'd
At that dread crisis to instruct thy mind
Things of eternal consequence to weigh,
And to thine heart just feelings to convey
Of things above, and of the future doom,
And what the births of the dread world to come.

From tossing seas I welcome thee to land.
"Resign her, *Nereid,*" 'twas thy God's command.
Thy spouse late buried, as thy fears conceiv'd,

Again returns, thy fears are all reliev'd:
Thy daughter blooming with superior grace
Again thou see'st, again thine arms embrace;
O come, and joyful show thy spouse his heir,
And what the blessings of maternal care!

✤✤✤✤✤✤✤

TO A LADY AND HER CHILDREN, ON THE DEATH OF HER SON AND THEIR BROTHER.

O'erwhelming sorrow now demands my song:
From death the overwhelming sorrow sprung.
What flowing tears? What hearts with grief opprest?
What sighs on sighs heave the fond parent's breast?
The brother weeps, the hapless sisters join
Th' increasing woe, and swell the crystal brine;
The poor, who once his gen'rous bounty fed,
Droop, and bewail their benefactor dead.
In death the friend, the kind companion lies,
And in one death what various comfort dies!

Th' unhappy mother sees the sanguine rill
Forget to flow, and nature's wheels stand still,
But see from earth his spirit far remov'd,
And know no grief recals your best-belov'd:
He, upon pinions swifter than the wind,
Has left mortality's sad scenes behind
For joys to this terrestial state unknown,
And glories richer than the monarch's crown.
Of virtue's steady course the prize behold!
What blissful wonders to his mind unfold!
But of celestial joys I sing in vain:
Attempt not, muse, the too advent'rous strain.

No more in briny show'rs, ye friends around,
Or bathe his clay, or waste them on the ground:
Still do you weep, still wish for his return?
How cruel thus to wish, and thus to mourn?

No more for him the streams of sorrow pour,
But haste to join him on the heav'nly shore,
On harps of gold to tune immortal lays,
And to your God immortal anthems raise.

✤✤✤✤✤✤✤

TO A GENTLEMAN AND LADY ON THE DEATH OF THE LADY'S BROTHER AND SISTER, AND A CHILD OF THE NAME AVIS, *AGED ONE YEAR.*

ON *Death's* domain intent I fix my eyes,
Where human nature in vast ruin lies:
With pensive mind I search the drear abode,
Where the great conqu'ror has his spoils, bestow'd;
There there the offspring of six thousand years
In endless numbers to my view appears:
Whole kingdoms in his gloomy den are thrust,
And nations mix with their primeval dust:
Insatiate still he gluts the ample tomb;
His is the present, his the age to come.
See here a brother, here a sister spread,
And a sweet daughter mingled with the dead.

But, *Madam,* let your grief be laid aside,
And let the fountain of your tears be dry'd,
In vain they flow to wet the dusty plain,
Your sighs are wafted to the skies in vain,
Your pains they witness, but they can no more,
While *Death* reigns tyrant o'er this mortal shore.

The glowing stars and silver queen of light
At last must perish in the gloom of night:
Resign thy friends to that Almighty hand,
Which gave them life, and bow to his command;
Thine *Avis* give without a murm'ring heart,
Though half thy soul be fated to depart.
To shining guards consign thine infant care

To waft triumphant through the seas of air:
Her soul enlarg'd to heav'nly pleasure springs,
She feeds on truth and uncreated things.
Methinks I hear her in the realms above,
And leaning forward with a filial love,
Invite you there to share immortal bliss
Unknown, untasted in a state like this.
With tow'ring hopes, and growing grace arise,
And seek beatitude beyond the skies.

✤✤✤✤✤✤✤

ON THE DEATH OF DR. SAMUEL MARSHALL. 1771.

THROUGH thickest glooms look back, immortal shade,
On that confusion which thy death has made;
Or from *Olympus'* height look down, and see
A *Town* involv'd in grief bereft of thee.
Thy *Lucy*[14] sees thee mingle with the dead,
And rends the graceful tresses from her head,
Wild in her woe, with grief unknown opprest
Sigh follows sigh deep heaving from her breast.

Too quickly fled, ah! whither art thou gone?
Ah! lost for ever to thy wife and son!
The hapless child, thine only hope and heir,
Clings round his mother's neck, and weeps his sorrows there.
The loss of thee on *Tyler's* soul returns,
And *Boston* for her dear physician mourns.

When sickness call'd for *Marshall's* healing hand,
With what compassion did his soul expand?
In him we found the father and the friend:
In life how lov'd! how honour'd in his end!

14. A Lucy Marshall became a member of Boston's Old South Church on August 18, 1771, at the same time that Phillis did (see *An Historical Catalogue of the Old South Church (Third Church) Boston,* published in Boston in 1883).

And must not then our *Æsculapius* stay
To bring his ling'ring infant into day?
The babe unborn in the dark womb is tost,
And seems in anguish for its father lost.

Gone is *Apollo* from his house of earth,
But leaves the sweet memorials of his worth:
The common parent, whom we all deplore,
From yonder world unseen must come no more,
Yet 'midst our woes immortal hopes attend
The spouse, the sire, the universal friend.

✤✤✤✤✤✤✤

TO A GENTLEMAN ON HIS VOYAGE TO GREAT-BRITAIN *FOR THE RECOVERY OF HIS HEALTH.*[15]

WHILE others chant the gay *Elysian* scenes,
Of balmy zephyrs, and of flow'ry plains,
My song more happy speaks a greater name,
Feels higher motives and a nobler flame.
For thee, O R–, the muse attunes her strings,
And mounts sublime above inferior things.

I sing not now of green embow'ring woods,
I sing not now the daughters of the floods,
I sing not of the storms o'er ocean driv'n,
And how they howl'd along the waste of heav'n,
But I to R– would paint the *British* shore,
And vast *Atlantic,* not untry'd before:

15. Daniel Ricketson, *The History of New Bedford* (New Bedford, 1858), p. 262, says that this poem is addressed to Joseph Rotch, a brother of William Rotch, Sr., both members of the prominent merchant family of the same name of New Bedford and Nantucket (pp. 108-12 and *passim*). "The fervent wish of the gentle Phillis was not granted. The subject of her invocation died in Bristol, England, soon after his arrival" (p. 263). (This poem is reprinted in Ricketson.) William Rotch places the date of his brother's death in 1767 ("Autobiographical Memoir of William Rotch," *The New-England Historical and Genealogical Register,* XXXII [April, 1878], pp. 154-55), thus giving us the distinct possibility that this was one of Phillis' earliest poems.

Thy life impair'd commands thee to arise,
Leave these bleak regions and inclement skies,
Where chilling winds return the winter past,
And nature shudders at the furious blast.

O thou stupendous, earth-enclosing main
Exert thy wonders to the world again!
If ere thy pow'r prolong'd the fleeting breath,
Turn'd back the shafts, and mock'd the gates of death,
If ere thine air dispens'd an healing pow'r,
Or snatch'd the victim from the fatal hour,
This equal case demands thine equal care,
And equal wonders may this patient share.
But unavailing, frantic is the dream
To hope thine aid without the aid of him
Who gave thee birth and taught thee where to flow,
And in thy waves his various blessings show.

May R— return to view his native shore
Replete with vigour not his own before,
Then shall we see with pleasure and surprise,
And own thy work, great Ruler of the skies!

✤✤✤✤✤✤✤

TO THE REV. DR. THOMAS AMORY ON READING HIS SERMONS ON DAILY DEVOTION, IN WHICH THAT DUTY IS RECOMMENDED AND ASSISTED.[16]

TO cultivate in ev'ry noble mind
Habitual grace, and sentiments refin'd,
Thus while you strive to mend the human heart,
Thus while the heav'nly precepts you impart,

16. Thomas Amory, D.D., (1701-1774), English minister and religious writer. The book referred to here is probably his *Daily Devotion Assisted and Recommended, In Four Sermons,* second edition (London, 1770; Boston, 1772).

O may each bosom catch the sacred fire,
And youthful minds to *Virtue's* throne aspire!

When God's eternal ways you set in sight,
And *Virtue* shines in all her native light,
In vain would *Vice* her works in night conceal,
For *Wisdom's* eye pervades the sable veil.

Artists may paint the sun's effulgent rays,
But *Amory's* pen the brighter God displays:
While his great works in *Amory's* pages shine,
And while he proves his essence all divine,
The Atheist sure no more can boast aloud
Of chance, or nature, and exclude the God;
As if the clay without the potter's aid
Should rise in various forms, and shapes self-made,
Or worlds above with orb o'er orb profound
Self-mov'd could run the everlasting round.
It cannot be—unerring *Wisdom* guides
With eye propitious, and o'er all presides.

Still prosper, *Amory!* still may'st thou receive
The warmest blessings which a muse can give,
And when this transitory state is o'er,
When kingdoms fall, and fleeting *Fame's* no more,
May *Amory* triumph in immortal fame,
A noble title, and superior name!

✤✤✤✤✤✤✤

ON THE DEATH OF J. C. AN INFANT.

NO more the flow'ry scenes of pleasure rise,
Nor charming prospects greet the mental eyes,
No more with joy we view that lovely face
Smiling, disportive, flush'd with ev'ry grace.

The tear of sorrow flows from ev'ry eye,
Groans answer groans, and sighs to sighs reply;
What sudden pangs shot thro' each aching heart,
When, *Death,* thy messenger dispatch'd his dart?

Thy dread attendants, all-destroying *Pow'r,*
Hurried the infant to his mortal hour.
Could'st thou unpitying close those radiant eyes?
Or fail'd his artless beauties to surprise?
Could not his innocence thy stroke controul,
Thy purpose shake, and soften all thy soul?

The blooming babe, with shades of *Death* o'er-
spread,
No more shall smile, no more shall raise its head,
But, like a branch that from the tree is torn,
Falls prostrate, wither'd, languid, and forlorn.
"Where flies my *James?*" 'tis thus I seem to hear
The parent ask, "Some angel tell me where
"He wings his passage thro' the yielding air?"
Methinks a cherub bending from the skies
Observes the question, and serene replies,
"In heav'ns high palaces your babe appears:
"Prepare to meet him, and dismiss your tears."
Shall not th' intelligence your grief restrain,
And turn the mournful to the chearful strain?
Cease your complaints, suspend each rising sigh,
Cease to accuse the Ruler of the sky.
Parents, no more indulge the falling tear:
Let *Faith* to heav'n's refulgent domes repair,
There see your infant, like a seraph glow:
What charms celestial in his numbers flow
Melodious, while the soul-enchanting strain
Dwells on his tongue, and fills th'ethereal plain?
Enough—for ever cease your murm'ring breath;
Not as a foe, but friend converse with *Death,*
Since to the port of happiness unknown
He brought that treasure which you call your own.
The gift of heav'n intrusted to your hand
Chearful resign at the divine command:
Not at your bar must sov'reign *Wisdom* stand.

AN HYMN TO HUMANITY. TO S. P. G. ESQ.[17]

I.

LO! for this dark terrestrial ball
Forsakes his azure-paved hall
    A prince of heav'nly birth!
Divine *Humanity* behold.
What wonders rise, what charms unfold
    At his descent to earth!

II.

The bosoms of the great and good
With wonder and delight he view'd,
    And fix'd his empire there:
Him, close compressing to his breast,
The sire of gods and men address'd,
    "My son, my heav'nly fair!

III.

"Descend to earth, there place thy throne;
"To succour man's afflicted son
    "Each human heart inspire:
"To act in bounties unconfin'd
"Enlarge the close contracted mind,
    "And fill it with thy fire."

IV.

Quick as the word, with swift career
He wings his course from star to star,
    And leaves the bright abode.
The *Virtue* did his charms impart;
Their G———! then thy raptur'd heart
    Perceiv'd the rushing God:

V.

For when thy pitying eye did see
The languid muse in low degree,
    Then, then at thy desire

17. Perhaps Samuel P. Gardner, Esq., known for his garden. (Reference: Justin Winsor, ed., *The Memorial History of Boston* [Boston, 1881], IV, 608, *n.* 3.)

Descended the celestial nine;
O'er me methought they deign'd to shine,
    And deign'd to string my lyre.

VI.

Can *Afric's* muse forgetful prove?
Or can such friendship fail to move
    A tender human heart?
Immortal *Friendship* laurel-crown'd
The smiling *Graces* all surround
    With ev'ry heav'nly *Art*.

❖❖❖❖❖❖❖

TO THE HONOURABLE T. H. ESQ; ON THE DEATH OF HIS DAUGHTER.[18]

WHILE deep you mourn beneath the cypress-shade
The hand of Death, and your dear daughter laid
In dust, whose absence gives your tears to flow,
And racks your bosom with incessant woe,
Let *Recollection* take a tender part,
Assuage the raging tortures of your heart,
Still the wild tempest of tumultuous grief,
And pour the heav'nly nectar of relief:
Suspend the sigh, dear Sir, and check the groan,
Divinely bright your daughter's *Virtues* shone:
How free from scornful pride her gentle mind,
Which ne'er its aid to indigence declin'd!
Expanding free, it sought the means to prove
Unfailing charity, unbounded love!

18. For the version of this poem published earlier (Jan. 2, 1773) as "To the Hon'ble Thomas Hubbard, Esq.; On the Death of Mrs. Thankfull Leonard," see Part Two, page 77. Thomas Hubbard (1702-1773) was for twenty years treasurer of Harvard College—a distinguished citizen and merchant, very active in public affairs. He was one of those who signed the letter "To The Public" which was printed at the front of the 1773 volume to attest to the personal knowledge that Phillis had been the author of the poems presented as hers. (Also see Phillis' earlier poem to Mrs. Leonard on the death of her husband, Thankfull, who is also twice referred to in this poem [p. 12].)

She unreluctant flies to see no more
Her dear-lov'd parents on earth's dusky shore:
Impatient heav'n's resplendent goal to gain,
She with swift progress cuts the azure plain,
Where grief subsides, where changes are no more,
And life's tumultuous billows cease to roar;
She leaves her earthly mansion for the skies,
Where new creations feast her wond'ring eyes.

To heav'n's high mandate chearfully resign'd
She mounts, and leaves the rolling globe behind;
She, who late wish'd that *Leonard* might return,
Has ceas'd to languish, and forgot to mourn;
To the same high empyreal mansions come,
She joins her spouse, and smiles upon the tomb:
And thus I hear her from the realms above:
"Lo! this the kingdom of celestial love!
"Could ye, fond parents, see our present bliss,
"How soon would you each sigh, each fear dismiss?
"Amidst unutter'd pleasures whilst I play
"In the fair sunshine of celestial day,
"As far as grief affects an happy soul
"So far doth grief my better mind controul,
"To see on earth my aged parents mourn,
"And secret wish for T—l to return:
"Let brighter scenes your ev'ning-hours employ:
"Converse with heav'n, and taste the promis'd joy."

✣✣✣✣✣✣✣

NIOBE IN DISTRESS FOR HER CHILDREN SLAIN BY APOLLO, FROM OVID'S METAMORPHOSES, BOOK VI. AND FROM A VIEW OF THE PAINTING OF MR. RICHARD WILSON.[19]

APOLLO'S wrath to man the dreadful spring
Of ills innum'rous, tuneful goddess, sing!

19. Welsh painter (1713-1782) noted for his landscapes. He used the Niobe story for three paintings, two of which were engraved during the time Phillis lived in Boston. It is uncertain which she refers to here.

Thou who did'st first th' ideal pencil give,
And taught'st the painter in his works to live,
Inspire with glowing energy of thought,
What *Wilson* painted, and what *Ovid* wrote.
Muse! lend thy aid, nor let me sue in vain,
Tho' last and meanest of the rhyming train!
O guide my pen in lofty strains to show
The *Phrygian* queen, all beautiful in woe.

'Twas where *Mæonia* spreads her wide domain
Niobe dwelt, and held her potent reign:
See in her hand the regal sceptre shine,
The wealthy heir of *Tantalus* divine,
He most distinguish'd by *Dodonean Jove,*
To approach the tables of the gods above:
Her grandsire *Atlas,* who with mighty pains
Th' ethereal axis on his neck sustains:
Her other grandsire on the throne on high
Rolls the loud-pealing thunder thro' the sky.

Her spouse, *Amphion,* who from *Jove* too springs,
Divinely taught to sweep the sounding strings.

Seven sprightly sons the royal bed adorn,
Seven daughters beauteous as the op'ning morn,
As when *Aurora* fills the ravish'd sight,
And decks the orient realms with rosy light
From their bright eyes the living splendors play,
Nor can beholders bear the flashing ray.

Wherever, *Niobe,* thou turn'st thine eyes,
New beauties kindle, and new joys arise!
But thou had'st far the happier mother prov'd,
If this fair offspring had been less belov'd:
What if their charms exceed *Aurora's* teint,
No words could tell them, and no pencil paint,
Thy love too vehement hastens to destroy
Each blooming maid, and each celestial boy.

Now *Manto* comes, endu'd with mighty skill,
The past to explore, the future to reveal.

Thro' *Thebes'* wide streets *Tiresia's* daughter came,
Divine *Latona's* mandate to proclaim:
The *Theban* maids to hear the orders ran,
When thus *Mœonia's* prophetess began:

"Go *Thebans!* great *Latona's* will obey,
"And pious tribute at her altars pay:
"With rights divine, the goddess be implor'd,
"Nor be her sacred offspring unador'd."
Thus *Manto* spoke. The *Theban* maids obey,
And pious tribute to the goddess pay.
The rich perfumes ascend in waving spires,
And altars blaze with consecrated fires;
The fair assembly moves with graceful air,
And leaves of laurel bind the flowing hair.

Niobe comes with all her royal race,
With charms unnumber'd, and superior grace:
Her *Phrygian* garments of delightful hue,
Inwove with gold, refulgent to the view,
Beyond description beautiful she moves
Like heav'nly *Venus,* 'midst her smiles and loves:
She views around the supplicating train,
And shakes her graceful head with stern disdain,
Proudly she turns around her lofty eyes,
And thus reviles celestial deities:
"What madness drives the *Theban* ladies fair
"To give their incense to surrounding air?
"Say why this new sprung deity preferr'd?
"Why vainly fancy your petitions heard?
"Or say why *Cœus'* offspring is obey'd,
"While to my goddesship no tribute's paid?
"For me no altars blaze with living fires,
"No bullock bleeds, no frank incense transpires,
"Tho' *Cadmus'* palace, not unknown to fame,
"And *Phrygian* nations all revere my name.
"Wher're I turn my eyes vast wealth I find.
"Lo! here an empress with a goddess join'd.
"What, shall a *Titaness* be deify'd,

"To whom the spacious earth a couch deny'd?
"Nor heav'n, nor earth, nor sea receiv'd your queen,
" 'Till pitying *Delos* took the wand'rer in.
"Round me what a large progeny is spread!
"No frowns of fortune has my soul to dread.
"What if indignant she decrease my train
"More than *Latona's* number will remain;
"Then hence, ye *Theban* dames, hence haste away,
"Nor longer off'rings to *Latona* pay;
"Regard the orders of *Amphion's* spouse,
"And take the leaves of laurel from your brows."
Niobe spoke. The *Theban* maids obey'd,
Their brows unbound, and left the rights unpaid.

The angry goddess heard, then silence broke
On *Cynthus'* summit, and indignant spoke;
"*Phœbus!* behold, thy mother in disgrace.
"Who to no goddess yields the prior place
"Except to *Juno's* self, who reigns above,
"The spouse and sister of the thund'ring *Jove.*
"*Niobe* sprung from Tantalus inspires
"Each *Theban* bosom with rebellious fires;
"No reason her imperious temper quells,
"But all her father in her tongue rebels;
"Wrap her own sons for her blaspheming breath,
"*Apollo!* wrap them in the shades of death."
Latona ceas'd and ardent thus replies,
The God whose glory decks th' expanded skies.

"Ceast thy complaints, mine be the task assign'd
"To punish pride, and scourge the rebel mind."
This *Phœbe* join'd.—They wing their instant flight;
Thebes trembled as th' immortal pow'rs alight.

With clouds incompass'd glorious *Phœbus* stands;
The feather'd vengeance quiv'ring in his hands.

Near *Cadmus'* walls a plain extended lay,
Where *Thebes'* young princes pass'd in sport the day:
There the bold coursers bounded o'er the plains,

While their great masters held the golden reins.
Ismenus first the racing pastime led,
And rul'd the fury of his flying steed.
"Ah me," he sudden cries, with shrieking breath,
While in his breast he feels the shaft of death;
He drops the bridle on his courser's mane,
Before his eyes in shadows swims the plain,
He, the first-born of great *Amphion's* bed,
Was struck the first, first mingled with the dead.

Then didst thou, *Sipylus,* the language hear
Of fate portentous whistling in the air:
As when th' impending storm the sailor sees
He spreads his canvas to the fav'ring breeze,
So to thine horse thou gav'st the golden reins,
Gav'st him to rush impetuous o'er the plains:
But ah! a fatal shaft from *Phœbus'* hand
Smites through thy neck, and sinks thee on the sand.

Two other brothers were at *wrestling* found,
And in their pastime claspt each other round:
A shaft that instant from *Apollo's* hand
Transfixt them both, and stretcht them on the sand:
Together they their cruel fate bemoan'd,
Together languish'd, and together groan'd:
Together too th' unbodied spirits fled,
And sought the gloomy mansions of the dead.

Alphenor saw, and trembling at the view,
Beat his torn breast, that chang'd its snowy hue.
He flies to raise them in a kind embrace;
A brother's fondness triumphs in his face:
Alphenor fails in this fraternal deed,
A dart dispatch'd him (so the fates decreed:)
Soon as the arrow left the deadly wound,
His issuing entrails smoak'd upon the ground.

What woes on blooming *Damasichon* wait!
His sighs portend his near impending fate.
Just where the well-made leg begins to be,

And the soft sinews form the supple knee,
The youth sore wounded by the *Delian* god
Attempts t' extract the crime-avenging rod,
But, whilst he strives the will of fate t' avert,
Divine *Apollo* sends a second dart;
Swift thro' his throat the feather'd mischief flies,
Bereft of sense, he drops his head, and dies.

Young *Ilioneus,* the last, directs his pray'r,
And cries, "My life, ye gods celestial! spare."
Apollo heard, and pity touch'd his heart,
But ah! too late, for he had sent the dart:
Thou too, O *Ilioneus,* art doom'd to fall,
The fates refuse that arrow to recal.

On the swift wings of ever-flying *Fame*
To *Cadmus'* palace soon the tidings came:
Niobe heard, and with indignant eyes
She thus express'd her anger and surprise:
"Why is such privilege to them allow'd?
"Why thus insulted by the *Delian* god?
"Dwells there such mischief in the pow'rs above?
"Why sleeps the vengeance of immortal *Jove?*"
For now *Amphion* too, with grief oppress'd,
Had plun'g the deadly dagger in his breast.
Niobe now, less haughty than before,
With lofty head directs her steps no more.
She, who late told her pedigree divine,
And drove the *Thebans* from *Latona's* shrine,
How strangely chang'd!—–yet beautiful in woe,
She weeps, nor weeps unpity'd by the foe.
On each pale corse the wretched mother spread
Lay overwhelm'd with grief, and kiss'd her dead,
Then rais'd her arms, and thus, in accents slow,
"Be sated cruel *Goddess!* with my woe;
"If I've offended, let these streaming eyes,
"And let this sev'nfold funeral suffice:
"Ah! take this wretched life you deign'd to save,
"With them I too am carried to the grave.

"Rejoice triumphant, my victorious foe,
"But show the cause from whence your triumphs flow?
"Tho' I unhappy mourn these childred slain,
"Yet greater numbers to my lot remain."
She ceas'd, the bow string twang'd with awful sound,
Which struck with terror all th' assembly round,
Except the queen, who stood unmov'd alone,
By her distresses more presumptuous grown.
Near the pale corses stood their sisters fair
In sable vestures and dishevell'd hair;
One, while she draws the fatal shaft away,
Faints, falls, and sickens at the light of day.
To sooth her mother, lo! another flies,
And blames the fury of inclement skies,
And, while her words a filial pity show,
Struck dumb——indignant seeks the shades below.
Now from the fatal place another flies,
Falls in her flight, and languishes, and dies.
Another on her sister drops in death;
A fifth in trembling terrors yields her breath;
While the sixth seeks some gloomy cave in vain,
Struck with the rest, and mingled with the slain.

One only daughter lives, and she the least;
The queen close clasp'd the daughter to her breast:
"Ye heav'nly pow'rs, ah spare me one," she cry'd,
"Ah! spare me one," the vocal hills reply'd:
In vain she begs, the Fates her suit deny,
In her embrace she sees her daughter die.

* "The queen of all her family bereft,
"Without or husband, son, or daughter left,
"Grew stupid at the shock. The passing air
"Made no impression on her stiff'ning hair.
"The blood forsook her face: amidst the flood
"Pour'd from her cheeks, quite fix'd her eye-balls stood.
"Her tongue, her palate both obdurate grew,
"Her curdled veins no longer motion knew;

* This Verse to the End is the Work of another Hand.

"The use of neck, and arms, and feet was gone,
"And ev'n her bowels hard'ned into stone:
"A marble statue now the queen appears,
"But from the marble steal the silent tears."

✤✤✤✤✤✤✤

TO S. M.[20] *A YOUNG* AFRICAN *PAINTER, ON SEEING HIS WORKS.*

TO show the lab'ring bosom's deep intent,
And thought in living characters to paint,
When first thy pencil did those beauties give,
And breathing figures learnt from thee to live,
How did those prospects give my soul delight,
A new creation rushing on my sight?
Still, wond'rous youth! each noble path pursue,
On deathless glories fix thine ardent view:
Still may the painter's and the poet's fire
To aid thy pencil, and thy verse conspire!
And may the charms of each seraphic theme
Conduct thy footsteps to immortal fame!
High to the blissful wonders of the skies
Elate thy soul, and raise thy wishful eyes.
Thrice happy, when exalted to survey
That splendid city, crown'd with endless day,
Whose twice six gates on radiant hinges ring:
Celestial *Salem*[21] blooms in endless spring.

20. Identified by Benjamin Brawley, *The Negro in Literature and Art,* (New York, 1934), p. 34, as Scipio Moorhead, "a young man who exhibited some talent for drawing and who was a servant of the Rev. John Moorhead of Boston." John Moorhead was born near Belfast, Ireland, was educated in Scotland, and came to Boston in 1727-28. For many years he was the pastor of a Presbyterian church in Boston which he established as the Church of the Presbyterian Strangers not long after his arrival. He remained in this work until after the Revolution, and he was one of those who signed the letter "To The Public" which was printed at the front of the 1773 volume to attest to the personal knowledge that Phillis had been the author of the poems presented as hers. Also see her elegy upon the death of the Rev. Mr. Moorhead, which is included in Part Two, page 79.

21. Not Salem, Massachusetts, but "Jerusalem"–i.e. Heaven.

Calm and serene thy moments glide along,
And may the muse inspire each future song!
Still, with the sweets of contemplation bless'd,
May peace with balmy wings your soul invest!
But when these shades of time are chas'd away,
And darkness ends in everlasting day,
On what seraphic pinions shall we move,
And view the landscapes in the realms above?
There shall thy tongue in heav'nly murmurs flow,
And there my muse with heav'nly transport glow:
No more to tell of *Damon's* tender sighs,
Or rising radiance of *Aurora's* eyes,
For nobler themes demand a nobler strain,
And purer language on th' ethereal plain.
Cease, gentle muse! the solemn gloom of night
Now seals the fair creation from my sight.

✤✤✤✤✤✤✤

TO HIS HONOUR THE LIEUTENANT-GOVERNOR,[22] *ON THE DEATH OF HIS LADY. MARCH 24, 1773.*

ALL-conquering Death! by thy resistless pow'r,
Hope's tow'ring plumage falls to rise no more!
Of scenes terrestial how the glories fly,
Forget their splendors, and submit to die!
Who ere escap'd thee, but the saint* of old
Beyond the flood in sacred annals told,
And the great sage,† whom fiery coursers drew
To heav'n's bright portals from *Elisha's* view;

22. Andrew Oliver (1731-1799), graduate of Harvard in 1749, judge and writer on political and scientific subjects, which publications gained him respect in both areas. He was a member of the American Academy and of the Philosophical Society. Oliver was primarily a loyalist, though he was known as a temperate and judicious man. He was one of those who signed the letter "To The Public" which was printed at the front of the 1773 volume to attest to the personal knowledge that Phillis had been the author of the poems presented as hers.

* Enoch.

† Elijah.

Wond'ring he gaz'd at the refulgent car,
Then snatch'd the mantle floating on the air.
From *Death* these only could exemption boast,
And without dying gain'd th' immortal coast.
Not falling millions sate the tyrant's mind,
Nor can the victor's progress be confin'd.
But cease thy strife with *Death,* fond *Nature,* cease:
He leads the *virtuous* to the realms of peace;
His to conduct to the immortal plains,
Where heav'n's Supreme in bliss and glory reigns.

There sits, illustrious Sir, thy beauteous spouse;
A gem-blaz'd circle beaming on her brows.
Hail'd with acclaim among the heav'nly choirs,
Her soul new-kindling with seraphic fires,
To notes divine she tunes the vocal strings,
While heav'n's high concave with the music rings.
Virtue's rewards can mortal pencil paint?
No—all descriptive arts, and eloquence are faint;
Nor canst thou, *Oliver,* assent refuse
To heav'nly tidings from the *Afric* muse.

As soon may change thy laws, eternal *fate,*
As the saint miss the glories I relate;
Or her *Benevolence* forgotten lie,
Which wip'd the trick'ling tear from *Mis'ry's* eye.
Whene'er the adverse winds were known to blow,
When loss to loss* ensu'd, and woe to woe,
Calm and serene beneath her father's hand
She sat resign'd to the divine command.

No longer then, great Sir, her death deplore,
And let us hear the mournful sigh no more,
Restrain the sorrow streaming from thine eye,
Be all thy future moments crown'd with joy!
Nor let thy wishes be to earth confin'd,
But soaring high pursue th' unbodied mind.
Forgive the muse, forgive th' advent'rous lays,
That fain thy soul to heav'nly scenes would raise.

* Three amiable Daughters who died when just arrived to Womens Estate.

A FAREWEL TO AMERICA. TO MRS. S. W.[23]

I.

ADIEU, *New-England's* smiling meads,
Adieu, the flow'ry plain:
I leave thine op'ning charms, O spring,
And tempt the roaring main.

II.

In vain for me the flow'rets rise,
And boast their gaudy pride,
While here beneath the northern skies
I mourn for *health* deny'd.

III.

Celestial maid of rosy hue,
O let me feel thy reign!
I languish till thy face I view,
Thy vanish'd joys regain.

IV.

Susannah mourns, nor can I bear
To see the crystal show'r,
Or mark the tender falling tear
At sad departure's hour;

V.

Not unregarding can I see
Her soul with grief opprest:
But let no sighs, no groans for me,
Steal from her pensive breast.

VI.

In vain the feather'd warblers sing,
In vain the garden blooms,
And on the bosom of the spring
Breathes out her sweet perfumes.

23. Almost certainly her mistress, Mrs. Susannah Wheatley, to whom she felt close ties. This poem obviously refers to Phillis' trip to England with Nathaniel Wheatley.

VII.

While for *Britannia's* distant shore
We sweep the liquid plain,
And with astonish'd eyes explore
The wide-extended main.

VIII.

Lo! *Health* appears! celestial dame!
Complacent and serene,
With *Hebe's* mantle o'er her Frame,
With soul-delighting mein.

IX.

To mark the vale where *London* lies
With misty vapours crown'd,
Which cloud *Aurora's* thousand dyes,
And veil her charms around.

X.

Why, *Phœbus,* moves thy car so slow?
So slow thy rising ray?
Give us the famous town to view,
Thou glorious king of day!

XI.

For thee, *Britannia,* I resign
New-England's smiling fields;
To view again her charms divine,
What joy the prospect yields!

XII.

But thou! Temptation hence away,
With all thy fatal train,
Nor once seduce my soul away,
By thine enchanting strain.

XIII.

Thrice happy they, whose heav'nly shield
Secures their souls from harm,
And fell *Temptation* on the field
Of all its pow'r disarms!

Boston, May 7, 1773.

A REBUS, BY I. B.[24]

I.

A BIRD delicious to the taste,
On which an army once did feast,
  Sent by an hand unseen;
A creature of the horned race,
Which *Britain's* royal standards grace;
  A gem of vivid green;

II.

A town of gaiety and sport,
Where beaux and beauteous nymphs resort,
  And gallantry doth reign;
A *Dardan* hero fam'd of old
For youth and beauty, as we're told,
  And by a monarch slain;

III.

A peer of popular applause,
Who doth our violated laws,
  And grievances proclaim.
Th' initials[25] show a vanquish'd town,
That adds fresh glory and renown
  To old *Britannia's* fame.

24. Although this was not written by Phillis, it was included in the 1773 volume and is included here because of her response, which follows it. It was probably written by James Bowdoin (see the poem on General Lee [p. 97] and the proposal for another volume of her poems [p. 111]). Bowdoin (1726-1790) was an important Revolutionary statesman and merchant, and a member of several learned societies (American and foreign). He became governor of Massachusetts in 1785. He was always actively interested in science and literature, was the first president of the American Academy of Arts and Sciences, and received honorary degrees from Harvard (from which he had graduated in 1745) and Edinburgh. (Bowdoin College is named for him.) He was one of those who signed the letter "To The Public" which was printed at the front of the 1773 volume to attest to the personal knowledge that Phillis had been the author of the poems presented as hers.

25. Of the answers to the six items above.

AN ANSWER TO THE REBUS, BY THE AUTHOR OF THESE POEMS.[26]

THE poet asks, and *Phillis* can't refuse
To shew th' obedience of the Infant muse.
She knows the *Quail* of most inviting taste
Fed *Israel's* army in the dreary waste;
And what's on *Britain's* royal standard borne,
But the tall, graceful, rampart *Unicorn?*
The *Emerald* with a vivid verdure glows
Among the gems which regal crowns compose;
Boston's a town, polite and debonair,
To which the beaux and beauteous nymphs repair,
Each *Helen* strikes the mind with sweet surprise,
While living lightning flashes from her eyes.
See young *Euphorbus* of the *Dardan* line
By *Menelaus'* hand to death resign:
The well known peer of popular applause
Is *C — m* zealous to support our laws.[27]
  Quebec now vanquish'd must obey,
  She too must annual tribute pay
  To *Britain* of immortal fame,
  And add new glory to her name.

FINIS.

26. See the preceding poem.
27. William Pitt, the Earl of Chatham, in general a friend to the colonies.

Part Two

✤✤✤✤✤✤✤

Miscellaneous Poems

TO THE UNIVERSITY OF CAMBRIDGE, WROTE IN 1767—[1]

While an intrinsic ardor bids me write
The muse doth promise to assist my pen.
'Twas but e'en now I left my native shore
The sable Land of error's darkest night.
There, sacred Nine! for you no place was found.
Parent of mercy, 'twas thy Powerful hand
Brought me in safety from the dark abode.
    To you, Bright youths! he points the height of
        Heav'n.
To you, the knowledge of the depths profound.
Above, contemplate the ethereal space
And glorious Systems of revolving worlds.
    Still more, ye sons of Science! you've receiv'd
The pleasing sound by messengers from heav'n,
The saviour's blood, for your redemption flows.
See Him, with hands stretched out upon the Cross!
Divine compassion in his bosom glows.
He hears revilers with oblique regard.
What Condescention in the Son of God!
When the whole human race by Sin had fal'n;
He deign'd to die, that they might rise again,
To live with him beyond the starry sky
Life without death, and Glory without End.———
    Improve your privileges while they stay:
Caress, redeem each moment, which with haste
Bears on its rapid wing Eternal bliss.
Let hateful vice so baneful to the Soul,
Be still avoided with becoming care;
Suppress the sable monster in its growth,
Ye blooming plants of human race, divine
An Ethiop tells you, tis your greatest foe

1. This is based on a photocopy of the original manuscript kindly supplied by the American Antiquarian Society, which has the manuscript. For the version of this poem published in the 1773 volume, see Part One, page 5. The date given for its composition makes this certainly one of her earliest poems, written when she was quite young.

Its transient sweetness turns to endless pain,
And brings eternal ruin on the Soul.

✤✤✤✤✤✤✤

ON THE DEATH OF THE REV'D DR. SEWALL. 1769.—[2]

E'er yet the morning heav'd its Orient head
Behold him praising with the happy dead.
Hail! happy Saint, on the immortal shore.
We hear thy warnings and advice no more:
Then let each one behold with wishful eyes
The saint ascending to his native skies,
From hence the Prophet wing'd his rapturous way
To mansions pure, to fair celestial day.——
　Then begging for the spirit of his God
And panting eager for the bless'd abode,
Let every one, with the same vigour soar
To bliss, and happiness, unseen before.
Then be Christ's image on our minds impress'd
And plant a saviour in each glowing Breast.
Thrice happy thou, arriv'd to glory at last,
What compensation for the evil past!
　Thou Lord, incomprehensible, unknown,
To Sense, we bow, at thy exalted Throne!
While thus we beg thy excellence to feel
Thy sacred spirit, in our hearts reveal
And make each one of us, that grace partake
Which thus we ask for the Redeemer's sake.

2. This is based on a photocopy of the original manuscript kindly supplied by the American Antiquarian Society, which has the manuscript. For the version of this poem published in the 1773 volume, see Part One, page 7. Sewall died on June 27, 1769, at the age of eighty-one. Note that Phillis spelled his name correctly in the manuscript. (In general, her handwriting is very even and pleasing.) The fact that she put in this manuscript a bracket to mark the couplet extended to a three-line rhyme leads one to believe that she was responsible for the frequent appearance of them in the 1773 volume.

"Sewall is dead." swift pinion'd fame thus cry'd.
"Is Sewall dead?" my trembling heart reply'd.
O what a blessing in thy flight deny'd!
But when our Jesus had ascended high,
With Captive bands he led Captivity;
And gifts receiv'd for such as knew not God.
Lord! find a Pastor, for thy Churche's
O ruin'd world! bereft of thee, we cry'd,
(The rocks responsive to the voice, reply'd.)
How oft for us this holy Prophet pray'd;
But ah! behold him in his Clay-cold bed.
By duty urg'd, my weeping verse to close,
I'll on his Tomb, an Epitaph compose.
Lo! here, a man bought with Christ's precious blood
Once a poor Sinner, now a Saint with God.———
Behold ye rich and poor, and fools and wise;
Nor let this monittor your hearts surprize!
I'll tell you all, what this great Saint has done
Which makes him Brighter[3] than the Glorious Sun.———
Listen ye happy from your seats above
I speak sincerely and with truth and Love.
He sought the Paths of virtue and of Truth
Twas this which made him happy in his Youth.
In Blooming years he found that grace divine
Which gives admittance to the sacred shrine.
Mourn him, ye Indigent, Whom he has fed,
Seek yet more earnest for the living Bread:
E'en Christ your Bread, who cometh from above
Implore his pity and his grace and Love.
Mourn him ye youth, whom he hath often told
God's bounteous Mercy from the times of Old.
I too, have cause this mighty loss to mourn
For this my monitor will not return.
Now this faint semblance of his life complete,
He is, thro' Jesus, made divinely great

3. In the manuscript the word "greater" is crossed through and replaced by "Brighter" written above it in the same handwriting.

And left a glorious pattern to repeat.
But when shall we, to this bless'd state arrive?
When the same graces in our hearts do thrive.

✤✤✤✤✤✤✤

AN ELEGIAC POEM,

On the DEATH of that celebrated Divine, and eminent Servant of JESUS CHRIST, the late Reverend, and pious GEORGE WHITEFIELD,[4]

Chaplain to the Right Honourable the Countess of Huntingdon, &c. &c.

Who made his Exit from this transitory
State, to dwell in the celestial Realms of Bliss, on LORD's-DAY, 30th of September, 1770, when he was seiz'd with a Fit of the Asthma, at NEWBURYPORT, near BOSTON, in NEW-ENGLAND. In which is a Condolatory Address to His truly noble Benefactress the worthy and pious Lady HUNTINGDON,—and the Orphan-Children in GEORGIA; who, with many Thousands, are left, by the Death of this great Man, to Lament the Loss of a Father, Friend, and Benefactor.
By PHILLIS, a Servant Girl of 17 Years of Age, Belonging to Mr. J. WHEATLEY, of Boston:—And has been but 9 Years in this Country from Africa.

Hail happy Saint on thy immortal throne!
To thee complaints of grievance are unknown;
We hear no more the music of thy tongue,
Thy wonted auditories cease to throng.
Thy lessons in unequal'd accents flow'd!
While emulation in each bosom glow'd;

4. Whitefield (1714-1770) was quite well known, and there were a number of special sermons and broadsides on the occasion of his death (reference: *Broadsides, Ballads, Etc. Printed in Massachusetts 1639-1800,* "Collections of the Massachusetts Historical Society," LXXV [Cambridge, Mass., 1922], 209-11), though Phillis' poem seems to have been reprinted more than the others. Whitefield was an evangelist and leader of Calvinistic methodism in Britain and America. He was much inter-

Thou didst, in strains of eloquence refin'd,
Inflame the soul, and captivate the mind.
Unhappy we, the setting Sun deplore!
Which once was splendid, but it shines no more;
He leaves this earth for Heaven's unmeasur'd height:
And worlds unknown, receive him from our sight;
There WHITEFIELD wings, with rapid course his way,
And sails to Zion, through vast seas of day.

When his AMERICANS were burden'd sore,
When streets were crimson'd with their guiltless gore!
Unrival'd friendship in his breast now strove:
The fruit thereof was charity and love
Towards *America*---couldst thou do more
Than leave thy native home, the *British* shore,
To cross the great Atlantic's wat'ry road,
To see *America's* distress'd abode?

---

ested in orphans and other unfortunates. However, while sympathetic with the plight of Negroes, he defended slavery on Biblical grounds.

This poem was first published in Boston in 1770 as a broadside. The *Massachusetts Spy* on October 11, 1770, advertised it as "this day published," but it may have been published even sooner. It was republished in 1770 as a broadside once in Newport, four more times in Boston, once in New York, and once in Philadelphia. It also appeared as an addendum to the printing of Ebenezer Pemberton's *Heaven the Residence of Saints,* a sermon on the death of Whitefield which was published in Boston and London in 1771; and a part of the poem was printed in 1812 in New Haven in John Gillies' *Memoirs of the Life of the Reverend George Whitefield, M.A.* (cited in the *Dictionary Catalog of the Schomburg Collection of Negro Literature and History* [Boston, 1962], IX, 8250). Further information about most of these can be found in Dorothy Porter, "Early American Negro Writings: A Bibliographical Study," *PBSA,* XXXIX (3rd Quarter 1945), 261-63.

For the 1773 version of this poem, see Part One, page 9. For another 1770 version, see the poem following this one. The version given here is based on a fold-out photocopy of a 1770 broadside in Charles F. Heartman, *Phillis Wheatley (Phillis Peters): A Critical Attempt and a Bibliography of Her Writings* (New York, 1915) and is apparently the original version, which was used in most of the early broadsides with only very minor variations which are probably printer's errors or changes. (Heartman's photocopy is of a broadside apparently in the Library Company of Philadelphia.) Its several reprintings gave Phillis her first fame as a poet. (Also see the Introduction and A Note on Text to this volume, the note to her poem to the Earl of Dartmouth [p. 33], and the dedication to the 1773 volume.)

Thy prayers, great Saint, and thy incessant cries,
Have pierc'd the bosom of thy native skies!
Thou moon hast seen, and ye bright stars of light
Have witness been of his requests by night!
He pray'd that grace in every heart might dwell:
He long'd to see *America* excell;
He charg'd its youth to let the grace divine
Arise, and in their future actions shine;
He offer'd THAT he did himself receive,

A greater gift not GOD himself can give:
He urg'd the need of HIM to every one;
It was no less than GOD's co-equal SON!
Take HIM ye wretched for your only good;
Take HIM ye starving souls to be your food.
Ye thirsty, come to his life giving stream:
Ye Preachers, take him for your joyful theme:
Take HIM, "my dear AMERICANS," he said,
Be your complaints in his kind bosom laid:
Take HIM ye *Africans,* he longs for you;
Impartial SAVIOUR, is his title due;
If you will chuse to walk in grace's road,
You shall be sons, and kings, and priests to GOD.

Great COUNTESS! we *Americans* revere
Thy name, and thus condole thy grief sincere:
We mourn with thee, that TOMB obscurely plac'd,
In which thy Chaplain undisturb'd doth rest.
New-England sure, doth feel the ORPHAN's smart;
Reveals the true sensations of his heart:
Since this fair Sun, withdraws his golden rays,
No more to brighten these distressful days!
His lonely *Tabernacle,* sees no more
A WHITEFIELD landing on the *British* shore:
Then let us view him in yon azure skies:
Let every mind with this lov'd object rise.
No more can he exert his lab'ring breath,
Seiz'd by the cruel messenger of death.
What can his dear AMERICA return?

But drop a tear upon his happy urn,
Thou tomb, shalt safe retain thy sacred trust,
Till life divine re-animate his dust.

Sold by EZEKIEL RUSSELL, in Queen-Street, and JOHN BOYLES, in Marlboro-Street.

✤✤✤✤✤✤✤

AN ODE OF VERSES[5]

On the much-lamented Death of the Rev. Mr. George Whitefield, Late Chaplain to the Countess of Huntingdon; *Who departed this Life, at* Newberry *near* Boston *in* New England, *on the Thirtieth of* September, *1770, in the Fifty-seventh Year of his Age. Compos'd in* America *by a Negro Girl Seventeen Years of Age, and sent over to a Gentleman of Character in* London.

HAIL Happy Saint, on thy Immortal Throne!
To thee Complaints of Grievance are unknown.
We hear no more the Music of thy Tongue,
Thy wonted Auditories cease to throng.
Thy Lessons in unequal'd Accents flow'd,
While Emulation in each Bosom glow'd.
Thou didst, in Strains of Eloquence refin'd,
Inflame the Soul, and captivate the Mind.
Unhappy we thy setting Sun deplore,
Which once was splendid, but it shines no more.
He leaves the Earth for Heaven's unmeasur'd Height,

5. This is based on a photocopy of a broadside in the Henry E. Huntington Library and Art Gallery. For the version of this poem printed in the 1773 volume, see Part One, page 9. The 1773 version differs from the earlier ones, most of which were quite similar in text, but with varying pictorial, typographical, and artistic embellishments to the individual broadsides. However, the version given here (apparently printed in England) seems to be unique, especially in that it seems to have been adapted to an English audience in the omission of twelve lines near the end of the usual version which primarily relate Whitefield to the Countess of Huntingdon and England, and in the addition of two quatrains and the Conclusion at the end. For the more typical Boston version, see the poem preceding this one.

And Worlds unknown receive him out of Sight.
There *Whitefield* wings with rapid Course his Way,
And sails to *Zion* thro' vast Seas of Day.
When his *Americans* were burthen'd sore,
When Streets were crimson'd with their guiltless Gore,
Wond'rous Compassion in his Breast now strove,
The Fruit thereof was Charity and Love.
Towards *America* what could he more!
Than leave his native Home, the *British* Shore,
To cross the Great *Atlantick* wat'ry Road,
To see *New England's* much-distress'd Abode.
Thy Prayers, great Saint, and thy incessant Cries,
Have often pierc'd the Bosom of the Skies.
Thou, Moon, hast seen, and thou, bright Star of Light.
Hast Witness been of his Requests by Night.
He pray'd for Grace in ev'ry Heart to dwell,
He long'd to see *America* excel.
He charg'd its Youth to let the Grace Divine
Arise, and in their future Actions shine.
He offer'd that he did himself receive:
A greater Gift not God himself could give.
He urg'd the Need of Him to ev'ry one,
It was no less than God's co-equal Son.
Take him, ye Wretched, for your only Good;
Take him, ye hungry Souls, to be your Food;
Take him, ye Thirsty, for your cooling Stream;
Ye Preachers, take him for your joyful Theme;
Take him, my dear *Americans,* he said,
Be your Complaints in his kind Bosom laid;
Take him, ye *Africans,* he longs for you,
Impartial Saviour is his Title due.
If you will walk in Grace's heavenly Road,
He'll make you free, and Kings, and Priests to God.
No more can he exert his lab'ring Breath,
Seiz'd by the cruel Messenger of Death.
What can his dear *America* return,
But drop a Tear upon his happy Urn.
Thou, Tomb, shalt safe retain thy sacred Trust,
Till Life Divine reanimate his Dust.

Our *Whitefield* the Haven has gain'd,
Outflying the Tempest and Wind;
His Rest he has sooner obtain'd,
And left his Companions behind.

With Songs let us follow his Flight,
And mount with his Spirit above;
Escap'd to the Mansions of Light,
And lodg'd in the *Eden* of Love.

THE CONCLUSION.

May *Whitefield's* Virtues flourish with his Fame,
And Ages yet unborn record his Name.
All Praise and Glory be to God on High,
Whose dread Command is, That we all must die.
To live to Life eternal, may we emulate
The worthy Man that's gone, e'er tis too late.

Printed and sold for the Benefit of a poor Family burnt out a few Weeks since near *Shoreditch Church*, that lost all they possessed, having nothing insur'd.

Price a Penny apiece, or 5 s. a Hundred to those that sell them again.

✤✤✤✤✤✤✤

TO MRS. LEONARD, ON THE DEATH OF HER HUSBAND.[6]

GRIM Monarch! see depriv'd of vital breath,
A young Physician in the dust of death!
Dost thou go on incessant to destroy:

6. This is based on a fold-out photocopy of the Boston 1771 broadside in Heartman, *Phillis Wheatley (Phillis Peters): A Critical Attempt and a Bibliography of Her Writings.* (Heartman's photocopy is of a broadside apparently in The Historical Society of Pennsylvania.) For the version of this poem published in the 1773 volume as "To a Lady on the Death of her Husband," see Part One, page 12. (Also see Phillis' poem to Hubbard on the death of his daughter [p. 46].)

The grief to double, and impair the joy?
Enough thou never yet wast known to say,
Tho' millions die thy mandate to obey.
Nor youth, nor science nor the charms of love,
Nor aught on earth thy rocky heart can move.
The friend, the spouse, from his dark realm to save,
In vain we ask the tyrant of the grave.

Fair mourner, there see thy own LEONARD spread,
Lies undistinguish'd from the vulgar dead;
Clos'd are his eyes, eternal slumbers keep,
His senses bound in never-waking sleep,
Till time shall cease; till many a shining world,
Shall fall from Heav'n, in dire confusion hurl'd:
Till dying Nature in wild torture lies;
Till her last groans shall rend the brazen skies!
And not till then, his active Soul shall claim,
Its body, now, of more than mortal frame.
But ah! methinks the rolling tears apace,
Pursue each other down the alter'd face.
Ah! cease ye sighs, nor rend the mourner's heart:
Cease thy complaints, no more thy griefs impart.
From the cold shell of his great soul arise!
And look above, thou native of the skies!
There fix thy view, where fleeter than the wind
Thy LEONARD flies, and leaves the earth behind.

Thyself prepare to pass the gloomy night,
To join forever in the fields of light;
To thy embrace, his joyful spirit moves,
To thee the partner of his earthly loves;
He welcomes thee to pleasures more refin'd
And better suited to the deathless mind.

TO THE AUTHOR OF THE LONDON MAGAZINE.[7]

Boston, in New-England, Jan. 1, 1772.

SIR,

As your Magazine is a proper repository for any thing valuable or curious, I hope you will excuse the communicating the following by one of your subscribers.

L.

There is in this town a young *Negro woman,* who left *her* country at ten years of age, and has been in *this* eight years. She is a compleat sempstress, an accomplished mistress of her pen, and discovers a most surprising genius. Some of her productions have seen the light, among which is a poem on the death of the Rev. Mr. George Whitefield.—The following was occasioned by her being in company with some young ladies of family, when one of them said she did not remember, among all the poetical pieces she had seen, ever to have met with a poem upon RECOLLECTION. The *African* (so let me call her, for so in fact she is) took the hint, went home to her master's, and soon sent what follows.

"MADAM,

"Agreeable to your proposing *Recollection* as a subject proper for me to write upon, I enclose these few thoughts upon it; and, as you was the first person who mentioned it, I thought none more proper to dedicate it to; and, if it

7. This letter and the accompanying poem appeared in the "Poetical Essays" section of *The London Magazine: Or, Gentleman's Monthly Intelligencer* for March, 1772, Vol. XLI, pp. 134-135. To the best of my knowledge it heretofore has been completely overlooked by others interested in Phillis Wheatley (although it is catalogued separately in the Schomburg Collection) and has never been reprinted. It is obviously an early version of the improved poem "On Recollection" in the 1773 volume (see Part One, page 28). The "A. M." of the dedication may have been Abigail May, who became a member of Boston's Old South Church in the same year that Phillis did—Abigail in February and Phillis in August of 1771. One is tempted to imagine the conversation which is cited in the letter and the resultant poem as being related to struggles with the catechism and the fervent preaching in Old South. This was Phillis' first magazine publication.

meets with your approbation, the poem is honoured, and the authoress satisfied. I am, Madam,

Your very humble servant,

PHILLIS."

RECOLLECTION.
To Miss A—— M——, humbly inscribed by the Authoress.

MNEME, begin; inspire, ye sacred Nine!
Your vent'rous *Afric* in the deep design.
Do ye rekindle the celestial fire,
Ye god-like powers! the glowing thoughts inspire,
Immortal Pow'r! I trace thy sacred spring,
Assist my strains, while I *thy* glories sing.
By *thee,* past acts of many thousand years,
Rang'd in due order, to the mind appears;
The *long-forgot* thy gentle hand conveys,
Returns, and soft upon the fancy plays.
Calm, in the visions of the night he pours
Th' exhaustless treasures of his secret stores.
Swift from above he wings his downy flight
Thro' *Phoebe's* realm, fair regent of the night.
Thence to the raptur'd poet gives his aid,
Dwells in his heart, or hovers round his head;
To give instruction to the lab'ring mind,
Diffusing light cœlestial and refin'd.
Still he pursues, unweary'd in the race,
And wraps his senses in the pleasing maze.
The Heav'nly Phantom *points* the actions done
In the past worlds, and tribes beneath the sun.
He, from his throne in ev'ry human breast,
Has *vice* condemn'd, and ev'ry *virtue* bless'd.
Sweet are the sounds in which thy words we hear,
Cœlestial musick to the ravish'd ear.

We hear thy voice, resounding o'er the plains,
Excelling Maro's sweet Menellian strains.
But awful *Thou!* to that perfidious race,
Who scorn thy warnings, nor the good embrace;
By *Thee* unveil'd, the horrid crime appears,
Thy mighty hand redoubled fury bears;
The time mis-spent augments their hell of woes,
While through each breast the dire contagion flows.
Now turn and leave the rude ungraceful scene,
And paint fair Virtue in immortal green.
For ever flourish in the glowing veins,
For ever flourish in poetick strains.
Be *Thy* employ to guide my early days,
And *Thine* the tribute of my youthful lays.
    Now **eighteen years* their destin'd course have run,
In due succession, round the central sun;
How did each folly unregarded pass!
But sure 'tis graven on eternal brass!
To *recollect,* inglorious I return;
'Tis mine past follies and past crimes to mourn.
The *virtue,* ah! unequal to the *vice,*
Will scarce afford small reason to rejoice.
    Such, RECOLLECTION! is thy pow'r, high-
        thron'd
In ev'ry breast of mortals, ever own'd.
The wretch, who dar'd the vengeance of the skies,
At last awakes with horror and surprise.
By *Thee* alarm'd, he sees impending fate,
He howls in anguish, and repents too late.
But oft *thy* kindness moves with timely fear
The furious rebel in his mad career.
Thrice bless'd the man, who in *thy* sacred shrine
Improves the REFUGE from the wrath divine.

* Her age.

TO THE REV. MR. PITKIN ON THE DEATH OF HIS LADY.[8]

WHERE Contemplation finds her sacred Spring;
Where heav'nly Music makes the Centre ring;
Where Virtue reigns unsulled, and divine;
Where Wisdom thron'd, and all the Graces shine;
There sits thy Spouse, amid the glitt'ring Throng;
There central Beauty feasts the ravish'd Tongue;
With recent Powers, with recent glories crown'd,
The Choirs angelic shout her Welcome round.
The virtuous Dead, demand a grateful Tear—
But cease thy Grief a-while, thy Tears forbear,
Not thine alone, the Sorrow I relate,
Thy blooming Off-spring feel the mighty Weight;
Thus, from the Bosom of the tender Vine,
The Branches torn, fall, wither, sink supine.
Now flies the Soul, tho' Æther unconfin'd.
Thrice happy State of the immortal Mind!
Still in thy Breast tumultuous Passions rise,
And urge the lucent Torrent from thine Eyes.
Amidst the Seats of Heaven, a Place is free
Among those bright angelic Ranks for thee.
For thee, they wait—and with expectant Eye,
Thy Spouse leans forward from th' ethereal Sky,
Thus in my Hearing, "Come away," she cries,
"Partake the sacred Raptures of the Skies!
"Our Bliss divine, to Mortals is unknown,
"And endless Scenes of Happiness our own;
"May the dear Off-spring of our earthly Love,
"Receive Admittance to the Joys above!
"Attune the Harp to more than mortal Lays,
"And pay with us, the Tribute of their Praise
"To Him, who died, dread Justice to appease,

8. This is based on a fold-out photocopy of the broadside in Heartman, *Phillis Wheatley (Phillis Peters): A Critical Attempt and a Bibliography of Her Writings.* (Heartman's photocopy is of a broadside apparently in The Historical Society of Pennsylvania.) For the version of this poem published in the 1773 volume as "To a Clergyman on the Death of his Lady," see Part One, page 24.

"Which reconcil'd, holds Mercy in Embrace;
"Creation too, her MAKER'S Death bemoan'd,
"Retir'd the Sun, and deep the Centre groan'd.
"He in his Death slew ours, and as he rose,
"He crush'd the Empire of our hated Foes.
"How vain their Hopes to put the GOD to flight,
"And render Vengence to the Sons of Light!"
Thus having spoke she turn'd away her Eyes,
Which beam'd celestial Radiance o'er the Skies.
Let Grief no longer damp the sacred Fire,
But rise sublime, to equal Bliss aspire;
Thy Sighs no more be wafted by the Wind,
Complain no more, but be to Heav'n resign'd.
'Twas thine to shew those Treasures all divine,
To sooth our Woes, the Task was also thine.
Now Sorrow is recumbent on thy Heart,
Permit the Muse that healing to impart,
Nor can the World, a pitying tear refuse,
They weep, and with them, ev'ry heavenly Muse.

Phillis Wheatley.

Boston, June 16th, 1772.

The above *Phillis Wheatley,* is a Negro Girl, about 18 Years old, who has been in this Country 11 Years.

✣✣✣✣✣✣✣

TO THE HON'BLE THOMAS HUBBARD, ESQ; ON THE DEATH OF MRS. THANKFULL LEONARD.[9]

WHILE thus you mourn beneath the Cypress shade
That hand of Death, a kind conductor made
To her whose flight commands your tears to flow

9. This is based on a fold-out photocopy of the broadside in Heartman, *Phillis Wheatley (Phillis Peters): A Critical Attempt and a Bibliography of Her Writings.* (Heartman's photocopy is of a broadside apparently in The Historical Society of Pennsylvania.) For the version of this poem published in the 1773 volume as "To the Honourable T. H. Esq.; on the Death of his Daughter," see Part One, page 46. (Also see Phillis' earlier poem to Mrs. Leonard on the death of her husband, Thankfull, who is referred to in this poem [p. 12].)

And wracks your bosom with a scene of wo:
Let Recollection bear a tender part
To sooth and calm the tortures of your heart:
To still the tempest of tumultous grief;
To give the heav'nly Nectar of relief;
Ah! cease, no more her unknown bliss bemoan!
Suspend the sigh, and check the rising groan.
Her virtues shone with rays divinely bright,
But ah! soon clouded with the shades of night.
How free from tow'ring pride, that gentle mind!
Which ne'er the hapless indigent declin'd,
Expanding free, it fought the means to prove
Unfailing Charity, unbounded Love!

She unreluctant flies, to see no more
Her much lov'd Parents on Earth's dusty shore,
'Till dark mortality shall be withdrawn,
And your bless'd eyes salute the op'ning morn.*
Impatient heav'n's resplendent goal to gain
She with swift progress scours the azure plain,
Where grief subsides, where passion is no more
And life's tumultous billows cease to roar,
She leaves her earthly mansions for the skies
Where new creations feast her won'dring eyes.
To heav'n's high mandate chearfully resign'd
She mounts, she flies, and leaves the rolling Globe
behind.
She who late sigh'd for LEONARD to return
Has ceas'd to languish, and forgot to mourn.
Since to the same divine dominions come
She joins her Spouse, and smiles upon the Tomb:
And thus addresses;— (let Idea rove) —
Lo! this the Kingdom of celestial Love!
Could our fond Parents view our endless Joy,
Soon would the fountain of their sorrows dry;
Then would delightful retrospect inspire,
Their kindling bosoms with the sacred fire!
Amidst unutter'd pleasures, whilst I play,

* Meaning the Resurrection.

In the fair sunshine of celestial day:
As far as grief affects a deathless Soul,
So far doth grief my better mind controul:
To see on Earth, my aged Parents mourn,
And secret, wish for THANKFULL to return!
Let not such thought their latest hours employ
But as advancing fast, prepare for equal Joy.

Boston, January 2. 1773. *Phillis Wheatley.*

✣✣✣✣✣✣✣

An ELEGY, To Miss. Mary Moorhead, on the DEATH of her Father, The Rev. Mr. JOHN MOORHEAD.[10]

Involv'd in Clouds of Wo, *Maria* mourns,
And various Anguish wracks her Soul by turns;
See thy lov'd Parent languishing in Death,
His Exit watch, and catch his flying Breath;
"Stay happy Shade," distress'd *Maria* cries;
"Stay happy Shade," the hapless Church replies;
"Suspend a while, suspend thy rapid flight,
"Still with thy Friendship, chear our sullen Night;
"The sullen Night of Error, Sin, and Pain;
"See Earth astonish'd at the Loss, complain;"
Thine, and the Church's Sorrows I deplore;
Moorhead is dead, and Friendship is no more;
From Earth she flies, nor mingles with our Wo,
Since cold the Breast, where once she deign'd to glow;
Here shone the heavenly Virtue, there confess'd,
Celestial Love, reign'd joyous in his Breast;
Till Death grown jealous for his drear Domain,

10. This is based on a photocopy of a broadside kindly supplied by the Massachusetts Historical Society, which has the original. This was the first poem published by Phillis after the publication of her 1773 book. (Also see her poem to S[cipio] M[oorhead] in Part One, page 54.) She apparently did not intend to include this poem in her next proposed book (see the proposal reprinted in the appendix).

Sent his dread Offspring, unrelenting Pain.
With hasty Wing, the Son of Terror flies,
Lest *Moorhead* find the Portal of the Skies;
Without a Passage through the Shades below,
Like great *Elijah,* Death's triumphant Foe;
Death follows soon nor leaves the Prophet long,
His Eyes are seal'd, and every Nerve unstrung;
Forever silent is the stiff'ning Clay,
While the rapt Soul, explores the Realms of Day.
Oft has he strove to raise the Soul from Earth,
Oft has he travail'd in the heavenly Birth;
Till JESUS took possession of the Soul,
Till the new Creature liv'd throughout the whole.
When fierce conviction seiz'd the Sinner's Mind,
The Law-loud thundering he to Death consign'd;
JEHOVAH'S Wrath revolving, he surveys,
The Fancy's terror, and the Soul's amaze.
Say, what is Death? The Gloom of endless Night,
Which from the Sinner, bars the Gates of Light:
Say, what is Hell? In Horrors passing strange;
His Vengeance views, who seals his final Change;
The winged Hours, the final Judgment brings,
Decides his fate, and that of Gods and Kings;
Tremendous Doom! And dreadful to be told,
To dwell in Tophet 'stead of shrines of Gold.
"Gods! Ye shall die like Men," the Herald cries,
"And stil'd no more the Children of the Skies."
Trembling he sees the horrid Gulf appear,
Creation quakes, and no Deliverer near;
With Heart relenting to his Feelings kind,
See *Moorhead* hasten to relieve his Mind.
See him the Gospel's healing Balm impart,
To sooth the Anguish of his tortur'd Heart.
He points the trembling Mountain, and the Tree,
Which bent beneath th' incarnate Deity,
How God descended, wonderous to relate,
To bear our Crimes, a dread enormous Weight;
Seraphic Strains too feeble to repeat,

Half the dread Punishment the GOD-HEAD meet.
Suspended there, (till Heaven was reconcil'd,)
Like *MOSES'* Serpent in the Desert wild.
The Mind appeas'd what new Devotion glows,
With Joy unknown, the raptur'd Soul o'erflows;
While on his GOD-like Savior's Glory bent,
His Life proves witness of his Heart's intent.
Lament ye indigent the Friendly Mind,
Which oft relented, to your Mis'ry kind.
With humble Gratitude he render'd Praise,
To Him whose Spirit had inspir'd his Lays;
To Him whose Guidance gave his Words to flow,
Divine instruction, and the Balm of Wo:
To you his Offspring, and his Church, be given,
A triple Portion of his Thirst for Heaven;
Such was the Prophet; we the Stroke deplore,
Which let's us hear his warning Voice no more.
But cease complaining, hush each murm'ring Tongue,
Pursue the Example which inspires my Song.
Let his Example in your Conduct shine;
Own the afflicting Providence, divine;
So shall bright Periods grace your joyful Days,
And heavenly Anthems swell your songs of Praise.

Boston, Decem. 15 1773. *Phillis Wheatley.*

Printed from the Original Manuscript, and Sold by WILLIAM M'ALPINE, at his Shop in *Marlborough-Street,* 1773.

✤✤✤✤✤✤✤

[*TO A GENTLEMAN OF THE NAVY.*][11]
For the ROYAL AMERICAN MAGAZINE

By particular request we insert the following Poem addressed, by Philis, (a young Affrican, *of surprising genius) to a gentleman of the navy, with his reply.*

11. This was the second periodical publication by Phillis, and it appeared in Boston in the "Poetical Essays" section of *The Royal Amer-*

By this single instance may be seen, the importance of education.—Uncultivated nature is much the same in every part of the globe. It is probable Europe *and* Affrica *would be alike* savage *or polite in the same circumstances; though, it may be questioned, whether men who have no* artificial *wants, are capable of becoming so ferocious as those, who, by faring* sumptuously every day, *are reduced to a habit of thinking it necessary to* their *happiness, to plunder the whole human race.*

---

ican Magazine, I (Dec., 1774), 473, 474. It was followed on pages 474 and 475 by a reply, which is also reprinted here, though it is not by Phillis. In the next number of the same magazine, she responded to that reply, which response is also reprinted here. Although these poems are cited in Vernon Loggins, *The Negro Author* (New York, 1931), to the best of my knowledge they have never been reprinted before.

In form, especially in syntax and punctuation, these are not very good poems. However, their subject matter is intriguing even though it is sporadic. Unfortunately, we know practically nothing about the context for these poems. Phillis apparently planned to include them in her next volume as "To Lieut R———— of the Royal Navy" followed by "To the same." (See the proposal reprinted in the appendix.) Perhaps some clue may be gained from the fact that she also planned to include in her next book a poem "To the Hon. John Montague Esq. Rear Admiral of the Blue," of the Royal Navy. Since Phillis does not seem to have been very certain of the spelling of the lieutenant's name, she might also have been unsure of the spelling of the name of the man she links with him. At any rate, it is of interest to note under Thursday, July 7, in the "Domestic Intelligence" section of the "Historical Chronicle" of *The Royal American Magazine* for July, 1774, (p. 269) two entries: "Sailed this day for England, in the ship Captain, Admiral Montague and family" and "Friday last arrived here from England, Vice Admiral Graves, in the Preston Man of War of fifty guns." Admiral Samuel Graves was replacing Montagu (Phillis again seems to have been incorrect in her spelling) as commander-in-chief of the North American Station, a post which Montagu had held since 1771. It is not cited in the *Dictionary of National Biography* that Graves had ever served along the cost of Africa, but several of his close relatives had, as had a great many of the men of the Royal Navy in the eighteenth century because of the trading done by the English in the Senegambia and Gold Coast areas (*e.g.,* see Eveline C. Martin, "The English Establishments on the Gold Coast in the Second Half of the Eighteenth Century," *Transactions of the Royal Historical Society,* 4th Series, V [1922], 167-208). Apparently, the lieutenant of these poems was attached to Graves' command, may have seen service on the coast of Africa, and was an admirer of Milton and Newton.

Celestial muse! for sweetness fam'd inspire
My wondrous theme with true poetic fire,
Rochfort, for thee! And Greaves deserve my lays
The sacred tribute of ingenuous praise.
For here, true merit shuns the glare of light,
She loves oblivion, and evades the sight.
At sight of her, see dawning genius rise
And stretch her pinions to her native skies.
Paris, for Helen's bright resistless charms,
Made Illion bleed and set the world in arms.
Had you appear'd on the Achaian shore
Troy now had stood, and Helen charm'd no more.
The Phrygian hero had resign'd the dame
For purer joys in friendship's sacred flame,
The noblest gift, and of immortal kind,
That brightens, dignifies the manly mind.
Calliope, half gracious to my prayer,
Grants but the half and scatters half in air.
Far in the space where ancient Albion keeps
Amidst the roarings of the sacred deeps,
Where willing forests leave their native plain,
Descend, and instant, plough the wat'ry main.
Strange to relate! with canvas wings they speed
To distant worlds; of distant worlds the dread.
The trembling natives of the peaceful plain,
Astonish'd view the heroes of the main,
Wond'ring to see two chiefs of matchless grace,
Of generous bosom, and ingenuous face,
From ocean sprung, like ocean foes to rest,
The thirst of glory burns each youthful breast.
In virtue's cause, the muse implores for grace,
These blooming sons of Neptune's royal race;
Cerulean youths! your joint assent declare,
Virtue to rev'rence, more than mortal fair,
A crown of glory, which the muse will twine,
Immortal trophy! Rochfort shall be thine!
Thine too O Greaves! for virtue's offspring share,
Celestial friendship and the muse's care.

Yours is the song, and your's the honest praise,
Lo! Rochfort smiles, and Greaves approves my lays.

BOSTON, October 30th, 1774.

✤✤✤✤✤✤✤

THE ANSWER.

Celestial muse! sublimest of the nine,
Assist my song, and dictate every line:
Inspire me once, nor with imperfect lays,
To sing this great, this lovely virgins praise:
But yet, alas! what tribute can I bring,
WH–TL–Y but smiles, whilst I thus faintly sing,
Behold with reverence, and with joy adore;
The lovely daughter of the Affric shore,
Where every grace, and every virtue join,
That kindles friendship and makes love divine;
In hue as diff'rent as in souls above;
The rest of mortals who in vain have strove,
Th'immortal wreathe, the muse's gift to share,
Which heav'n reserv'd for this angelic fair.
Blest be the guilded shore,[12] the happy land,
Where spring and autumn gently hand in hand;
O'er shady forests that scarce know a bound,
In vivid blaze alternately dance round:
Where cancers torrid heat the soul inspires;
With strains divine and true poetic fires;
(Far from the reach of Hudson's chilly bay)
Where cheerful phoebus makes all nature gay;
Where sweet refreshing breezes gently fan;
The flow'ry path, the ever verdent lawn,
The artless grottos, and the soft retreats;
"At once the lover and thee muse's seats."
Where nature taught, (tho' strange it is to tell,)
Her flowing pencil Europe to excell.
Britania's glory long hath fill'd the skies;

12. The Gold Coast.

Whilst other nations, tho' with envious eyes,
Have view'd her growing greatness, and the rules,
That's long been taught in her untainted schools:
Where great Sir Isaac! whose immortal name;
Still shines the brightest on the seat of fame;
By ways and methods never known before;
The sacred depth of nature did explore:
And like a God, on philosophic wings;
Rode with the planets thro' their circling rings:
Surveying nature with a curious eye,
And viewing other systems in the sky.
Where nature's bard with true poetic lays,
The pristine state of paradise displays,
And with a genius that's but very rare
Describes the first the only happy pair
That in terrestial mansions ever reign'd,
View'd happiness now lost, and now regain'd,
Unravel'd all the battles of the Gods,
And view'd old night below the antipodes.
On his imperious throne, with awful sway,
Commanding regions yet unknown today,
Or where those lofty bards have dwelt so long,
That ravish'd Europe with their heavenly song,
But now this blissful clime, this happy land,[13]
That all the neighbouring nations did command;
Whose royal navy neptunes waves did sweep,
Reign'd Prince alone, and sov'reign of the deep:
No more can boast, but of the power to kill,
By force of arms, or diabolic skill.
For softer strains we quickly must repair
To Wheatly's song, for Wheatly is the fair;
That has the art, which art could ne'er acquire:
To dress each sentence with seraphic fire.
Her wondrous virtues I could ne'er express!
To paint her charms, would only make them less.

December 2nd, 1774

13. England.

PHILIS's Reply to the Answer in our last by the Gentleman in the Navy[14]

For one bright moment, heavenly goddess! shine,
Inspire my song and form the lays divine.
Rochford, attend. Beloved of Phoebus! hear,
A truer sentence never reach'd thine ear;
Struck with thy song, each vain conceit resign'd
A soft affection seiz'd my grateful mind,
While I each golden sentiment admire
In thee, the muse's bright celestial fire.
The generous plaudit 'tis not mine to claim,
A muse untutor'd, and unknown to fame.
The heavenly sisters pour thy notes along
And crown their bard with every grace of song.
My pen, least favour'd by the tuneful nine,
Can never rival, never equal thine;
Then fix the humble Afric muse's seat
At British Homer's and Sir Isaac's feet.[15]
Those bards whose fame in deathless strains arise
Creation's boast, and fav'rites of the skies.
In fair description are thy powers display'd
In artless grottos, and the sylvan shade;
Charm'd with thy painting, how my bosom burns!
And pleasing Gambia on my soul returns,
With native grace in spring's luxuriant reign,
Smiles the gay mead, and Eden blooms again,
The various bower, the tuneful flowing stream,
The soft retreats, the lovers golden dream,
Her soil spontaneous, yields exhaustless stores;
For phoebus revels on her verdant shores.
Whose flowery births, a fragrant train appear,
And crown the youth throughout the smiling year,
There, as in Britain's favour'd isle, behold
The bending harvest ripen into gold!

14. This was the third periodical publication by Phillis, and it appeared in the "Poetical Essays" section of *The Royal American Magazine,* II (Jan., 1775), 34, 35, published in Boston. (See the two preceding poems.)

15. Milton and Newton.

Just are thy views of Afric's blissful plain,
On the warm limits of the land and main.
  Pleas'd with the theme, see sportive fancy play,
In realms devoted to the God of day! [16]
  Europa's bard, who the great depth explor'd,
Of nature, and thro' boundless systems soar'd,
Thro' earth, thro' heaven, and hell's profound domain,
Where night eternal holds her awful reign.
But, lo! in him Britania's prophet dies,
And whence, ah! whence, shall other *Newton's* rise?
Muse, bid thy Rochford's matchless pen display
The charms of friendship in the sprightly lay.
Queen of his song, thro' all his numbers shine,
And plausive glories, goddess! shall be thine.
With partial grace thou mak'st his verse excel,
And *his* the glory to describe so well.
Cerulean bard! to thee these strains belong,
The Muse's darling and the prince of song.

DECEMBER 5th, 1774.

✣✣✣✣✣✣✣

TO HIS EXCELLENCY GENERAL WASHINGTON.

The following LETTER and VERSES, *were written by the famous* Phillis Wheatley, *The African Poetess, and presented to his Excellency* Gen. Washington.[17]

16. One should be cautious in being tempted to use the preceding lines and her reference to Gambia as specific evidence for her homeland. It was the "Gentleman in the Navy" who introduced the topic of Africa in the preceding poem. What she says may be a poetic pose in reaction to his poem. On the other hand, even though she was rather young when taken from Africa, current events and the recent death of Mrs. Wheatley probably made such reminiscence—even under someone else's instigation—more attractive than it might have been otherwise.

17. This poem and letter were first printed in the "Poetical Essays" section of *The Pennsylvania Magazine,* II (April, 1776), 193, while Thomas Paine was its editor. She had planned to include it in her

SIR.

I Have taken the freedom to address your Excellency in the enclosed poem, and entreat your acceptance, though I am

---

next book (see the "Proposals" printed in the appendix). In a letter to Colonel Joseph Reed, his former secretary, dated Cambridge, 10 February 1776—which letter begins with a concern over the public's opinion of him—Washington says: "I recollect nothing else worth giving you the trouble of, unless you can be amused by reading a letter and poem addressed to me by Miss Phillis Wheatley. In searching over a parcel of papers the other day, in order to destroy such as were useless, I brought it to light again. At first, with a view of doing justice to her poetical genius, I had a great mind to publish the poem; but not knowing whether it might not be considered rather as a mark of my own vanity, than as a compliment to her, I laid it aside, till I came across it again in the manner just mentioned" (Jared Sparks, ed., *The Writings of George Washington* [Boston, 1834], III, 288). Washington apparently included the poem and letter, and since Reed was in Philadelphia at this time, it was probably through him that they reached *The Pennsylvania Magazine.* From Cambridge on February 28, 1776, Washington wrote the following reply: "Miss Phillis, Your favor of the 26th of October did not reach my hands, till the middle of December. Time enough, you will say, to have given an answer ere this. Granted. But a variety of important occurrences, continually interposing to distract the mind and withdraw the attention, I hope will apologize for the delay, and plead my excuse for the seeming but not real neglect. I thank you most sincerely for your polite notice of me, in the elegant lines you enclosed; and however undeserving I may be of such encomium and panegyric, the style and manner exhibit a striking proof of your poetical talents; in honor of which, and as a tribute justly due to you, I would have published the poem, had I not been apprehensive, that, while I only meant to give the world this new instance of your genius, I might have incurred the imputation of vanity. This, and nothing else, determined me not to give it place in the public prints. [new paragraph] If you should ever come to Cambridge, or near head-quarters, I shall be happy to see a person so favored by the Muses, and to whom nature has been so liberal and beneficent in her dispensations. I am, with great respect, your obedient humble servant" (Sparks, III, 297-98). Note that Washington was still not planning publication of the poem and probably had no direct responsibility in its being published. Sparks says in a note to the above letter that he could not find the letter and poem in Washington's correspondence and presumes them lost. As mentioned above, Washington had apparently sent them to Reed. Phillis accepted Washington's invitation that same year and was courteously received. It has been pointed out that her use of the term "Columbia" for her country in this poem may be the first use of the term with this meaning in print in America (George H. Moore, "The Name 'Columbia,'" *Proceedings of the Massachusetts Historical Society,* 2nd Series, II [1885-86], 163). This was Phillis' fourth periodical publication.

not insensible of its inaccuracies. Your being appointed by the Grand Continental Congress to be Generalissimo of the armies of North America, together with the fame of your virtues, excite sensations not easy to suppress. Your generosity, therefore, I presume, will pardon the attempt. Wishing your Excellency all possible success in the great cause you are so generously engaged in. I am,

Your Excellency's most obedient humble servant,
PHILLIS WHEATLEY.

Providence, Oct. 26, 1775.
His Excellency Gen. Washington.

Celestial choir! enthron'd in realms of light,
  Columbia's scenes of glorious toils I write.
While freedom's cause her anxious breast alarms,
She flashes dreadful in refulgent arms.
See mother earth her offspring's fate bemoan,
And nations gaze at scenes before unknown!
See the bright beams of heaven's revolving light
Involved in sorrows and the veil of night!
  The goddess comes, she moves divinely fair,
Olive and laurel binds her golden hair:
Wherever shines this native of the skies,
Unnumber'd charms and recent graces rise.
  Muse! bow propitious while my pen relates
How pour her armies through a thousand gates,
As when Eolus heaven's fair face deforms,
Enwrapp'd in tempest and a night of storms;
Astonish'd ocean feels the wild uproar,
The refluent surges beat the sounding shore;
Or thick as leaves in Autumn's golden reign,[18]
Such, and so many, moves the warrior's train.
In bright array they seek the work of war,
Where high unfurl'd the ensign waves in air.
Shall I to Washington their praise recite?
Enough thou know'st them in the fields of fight.
Thee, first in peace and honours,—we demand

18. Cf. John Milton, *Paradise Lost,* Bk. I, lines 301-302: "His [Satan's] legions . . ./Thick as autumnal leaves that strew the brooks . . . ."

The grace and glory of thy martial band.
Fam'd for thy valour, for thy virtues more,
Hear every tongue thy guardian aid implore!
 One century scarce perform'd its destined round,
When Gallic powers Columbia's fury found;
And so may you, whoever dares disgrace
The land of freedom's heaven-defended race!
Fix'd are the eyes of nations on the scales,
For in their hopes Columbia's arm prevails.
Anon Britannia droops the pensive head,
While round increase the rising hills of dead.
Ah! cruel blindness to Columbia's state!
Lament thy thirst of boundless power too late.
 Proceed, great chief, with virtue on thy side,
Thy ev'ry action let the goddess guide.
A crown, a mansion, and a throne that shine,
With gold unfading, WASHINGTON! be thine.

✤✤✤✤✤✤✤

AN ELEGY, SACRED TO THE MEMORY OF THAT GREAT DIVINE, THE REVEREND AND LEARNED DR. SAMUEL COOPER,[19]

Who departed this life December 29, 1783,
AETATIS 59.
BY PHILLIS PETERS.
BOSTON: Printed and Sold by E. Russell,
in Essex-Street, near Liberty-Pole,
M,DCC,LXXXIV.

19. This was first published in an eight-page pamphlet which included at the end the anthem used at Cooper's funeral on January 2, 1784. This reprinting is based on a photocopy of that pamphlet kindly supplied by the Massachusetts Historical Society, which has the original. It is one of only two poems to which Phillis signed her married name. (See the two poems following this one.) Cooper was graduated from Harvard in 1743 and was minister at the same church from 1746 until his death. He was a whig, a scholar, an attractive and popular preacher,

To the CHURCH and CONGREGATION
assembling in Brattle-Street, the following
ELEGY,
Sacred to the MEMORY of their late
Reverend and Worthy PASTOR, Dr.
SAMUEL COOPER, is, with
the greatest Sympathy, most respectfully
inscribed by their Obedient,
Humble Servant,
PHILLIS PETERS.

BOSTON, Jan. 1784.

O THOU whose exit wraps in boundless woe,
For Thee the tears of various Nations flow:
For Thee the floods of various sorrows rise
From the full heart and burst from streaming eyes,
Far from our view to Heaven's eternal height,
The Seat of bliss divine, and glory bright;
Far from the restless turbulence of life,
The war of factions, and impassion'd strife.
From every ill mortality endur'd,
Safe in celestial *Salem's* walls secur'd.

E'ER yet from this terrestrial state retir'd,
The Virtuous lov'd Thee, and the Wife admir'd.
The gay approv'd Thee, and the grave rever'd;
And all thy words with rapt attention heard!
The Sons of Learning on thy lessons hung,
While soft persuasion mov'd th' illit'rate throng.
Who, drawn by rhetoric's commanding laws,
Comply'd obedient, nor conceiv'd the cause.
Thy every sentence was with grace inspir'd,
And every period with devotion fir'd;

---

one interested in public affairs, a frequent contributor to the newspapers, a friend and correspondent of Franklin, a friend to literature, a patron to Harvard, one of the founders of the American Academy, and one of those who signed the letter "To The Public" which was printed at the front of the 1773 volume to attest to the personal knowledge that Phillis had been the author of the poems presented as hers. (For another poem on Cooper's death in the same vein, see *The Boston Magazine* for January, 1784, pp. 114-15.)

Bright Truth thy guide without a dark disguise,
And penetration's all-discerning eyes.

THY COUNTRY mourns th' afflicting Hand divine
That now forbids thy radiant lamp to shine,
Which, like the sun, resplendent source of light
Diffus'd its beams, and chear'd our gloom of night.

WHAT deep-felt sorrow in each *Kindred* breast
With keen sensation rends the heart distress'd!
Fraternal love sustains a tenderer part,
And mourns a BROTHER with a BROTHER'S heart.

THY CHURCH laments her faithful PASTOR fled
To the cold mansions of the silent dead.
There hush'd forever, cease the heavenly strain,
That wak'd the soul, but here resounds in vain.
Still live thy merits, where thy name is known,
As the sweet Rose, its blooming beauty gone
Retains its fragrance with a long perfume:
Thus COOPER! thus thy death-less name shall bloom
Unfading, in thy *Church* and *Country's* love,
While Winter frowns, or spring renews the grove.
The hapless Muse, her loss in COOPER mourns,
And as she sits, she writes, and weeps, by turns;
A Friend sincere, whose mild indulgent grace
Encourag'd oft, and oft approv'd her lays.

WITH all their charms, terrestrial objects strove,
But vain their pleasures to attract his love.
Such COOPER was—at Heaven's high call he flies;
His task well finish'd, to his native skies.
Yet to his fate reluctant we resign,
Tho' our's to copy conduct such as thine:
Such was thy wish, th' observant Muse survey'd
Thy latest breath, and this advice convey'd.

LIBERTY AND PEACE, A POEM.[20]

By Phillis Peters.
Boston:
Printed by WARDEN and RUSSELL,
At Their Office in Marlborough-Street.
M,DCC,LXXXIV.

LO! Freedom comes. Th' prescient Muse foretold,
All Eyes th' accomplish'd Prophecy behold:
Her Port describ'd, *"She moves divinely fair,*
"Olive and Laurel bind her golden Hair."
She, the bright Progeny of Heaven, descends,
And every Grace her sovereign Step attends;
For now kind Heaven, indulgent to our Prayer,
In smiling *Peace* resolves the Din of *War.*
Fix'd in *Columbia* her illustrious Line,
And bids in thee her future Councils shine.
To every Realm her Portals open'd wide,
Receives from each the full commercial Tide.
Each Art and Science now with rising Charms
Th' expanding Heart with Emulation warms.
E'en great *Britannia* sees with dread Surprize,
And from the dazzl'ing Splendor turns her Eyes!
Britain, whose Navies swept th' *Atlantic* o'er,
And Thunder sent to every distant Shore:
E'en thou, in Manners cruel as thou art,
The Sword resign'd, resume the friendly Part!
For *Galia's* Power espous'd *Columbia's* Cause,
And new-born *Rome* shall give *Britannia* Law,
Nor unremember'd in the grateful Strain,
Shall princely *Louis'* friendly Deeds remain;

20. The poem "Liberty and Peace" was first published as a four-page pamphlet in 1784. This is based on a photocopy of the pamphlet kindly supplied by The New-York Historical Society, which has the original. This is one of only two poems which Phillis signed with her married name (see the poems preceding and following this one). Note the continued use of the term "Columbia" and that in lines 3-4 she quotes her own description of Columbia from her poem to Washington, lines 9-10 (see page 89).

The generous Prince th' impending Vengeance eye's,
Sees the fierce Wrong, and to the rescue flies.
Perish that Thirst of boundless Power, that drew
On *Albion's* Head the Curse to Tyrants due.
But thou appeas'd submit to Heaven's decree,
That bids this Realm of Freedom rival thee!
Now sheathe the Sword that bade the Brave attone
With guiltless Blood for Madness not their own.
Sent from th' Enjoyment of their native Shore
Ill-fated—never to behold her more!
From every Kingdom on *Europa's* Coast
Throng'd various Troops, their Glory, Strength and Boast.
With heart-felt pity fair *Hibernia* saw
Columbia menac'd by the Tyrant's Law:
On hostile Fields fraternal Arms engage,
And mutual Deaths, all dealt with mutual Rage;
The Muse's Ear hears mother Earth deplore
Her ample Surface smoak with kindred Gore:
The hostile Field destroys the social Ties,
And ever-lasting Slumber seals their Eyes.
Columbia mourns, the haughty Foes deride,
Her Treasures plunder'd, and her Towns destroy'd:
Witness how *Charlestown's* curling Smoaks arise,
In sable Columns to the clouded Skies!
The ample Dome, high-wrought with curious Toil,
In one sad Hour the savage Troops despoil.
Descending *Peace* and Power of War confounds;
From every Tongue celestial *Peace* resounds:
As for the East th' illustrious King of Day,
With rising Radiance drives the Shades away,
So Freedom comes array'd with Charms divine,
And in her Train Commerce and Plenty shine.
Britannia owns her Independent Reign,
Hibernia, Scotia, and the Realms of *Spain*;
And great *Germania's* ample Coast admires
The generous Spirit that *Columbia* fires.
Auspicious Heaven shall fill with fav'ring Gales,

Where e'er *Columbia* spreads her swelling Sails:
To every Realm shall *Peace* her Charms display,
And Heavenly *Freedom* spread her golden Ray.

✤✤✤✤✤✤✤

TO MR. AND MRS.———, ON THE DEATH OF THEIR INFANT SON,

By Phillis Wheatley.[21]

O DEATH! whose sceptre, trembling realms obey,
And weeping millions mourn thy savage sway;
Say, shall we call thee by the name of friend,
Who blasts our joys, and bids our glories end?
Behold, a child who rivals op'ning morn,
When its first beams the eastern hills adorn;
So sweetly blooming once that lovely boy,
His father's hope, his mother's only joy,
Nor charms nor innocence prevail to save,
From the grim monarch of the gloomy grave!
Two moons revolve when lo! among the dead
The beauteous infant lays his weary head:
For long he strove the tyrant to withstand,
And the dread terrors of his iron hand;

21. This, Phillis' fifth periodical publication, appeared in the "Poetical Essays" section of *The Boston Magazine* in September, 1784, on page 488, only a few months before her own death and that of her last living child. It was the last thing written by her published during her lifetime. Although it is cited in Loggins, to the best of my knowledge this is the first time it has been reprinted. There was an editorial note on page 462 of this same number of *The Boston Magazine* which read as follows: "The Poem, in page 488, of this Number, was selected from a manuscript Volume of Poems, written by PHILLIS PETERS, formerly PHILLIS WHEATLEY—and is inserted as a Specimen of her Work: should this gain the Approbation of the Publick, and sufficient encouragement be given, a Volume will be shortly Published, by the Printers hereof, who receive subscriptions for said Work." (Greenleaf and Freeman were listed as the printers and publishers of the magazine.) Unfortunately, Phillis died in December. The proposed book was never published, proving to be the second attempt for a second volume of her poems which was not successful (see the first proposal reprinted in the appendix to this volume).

Vain was his strife, with the relentless power,
His efforts weak; and this his mortal hour;
He sings—he dies—celestial muse, relate,
His spirit's entrance at the sacred gate.
Methinks I hear the heav'nly courts resound,
The recent theme inspires the choirs around.
His guardian angel with delight unknown,
Hails his bless'd charge on his immortal throne;
His heart expands at scenes unknown before,
Dominions praise, and prostrate throngs adore;
Before the Eternal's feet their crowns are laid,
The glowing seraph vails his sacred head.
Spirits redeem'd, that more than angels shine,
For nobler praises tune their harps divine:
These saw his entrance; his soft hand they press'd,
Sat on his throne, and smiling thus address'd,
"Hail: thou! thrice welcome to this happy shore,
Born to new life where changes are no more;
Glad heaven receives thee, and thy God bestows,
Immortal youth exempt from pain and woes.
Sorrow and sin, those foes to human rest,
Forever banish'd from thy happy breast."
Gazing they spoke, and raptur'd thus replies,
The beauteous stranger in the etherial skies,
"Thus safe conducted to your bless'd abodes,
With sweet surprize I mix among the Gods;
The vast profound of this amazing grace,
Beyond your search, immortal powers, I praise;
Great Sire, I sing thy boundless love divine,
Mine is the bliss, but all the glory thine."
All heav'n rejoices as your . . . . sings,
To heavenly airs he tunes the sounding strings;
Mean time on earth the hapless parents mourn,
"Too quickly fled, ah! never to return."
Thee, the vain visions of the night restore,
Illusive fancy paints the phantom o'er;
Fain would we clasp him, but he wings his flight;
Deceives our arms, and mixes with the night;

But oh! suppress the clouds of grief that roll,
Invading peace, and dark'ning all the soul.
Should heaven restore him to your arms again,
Oppress'd with woes, a painful endless train,
How would your prayers, your ardent wishes, rise,
Safe to repose him in his native skies.

✤✤✤✤✤✤✤

ON THE CAPTURE OF GENERAL LEE.[22]

The following thoughts on his Excellency Major General Lee being betray'd into the hands of the Enemy by the treachery of a pretended Friend; To the Honourable James Bowdoin Esqr. are most respectfully Inscrib'd, By his most obedient and devoted humble servant,

PHILLIS WHEATLEY.

The deed perfidious, and the Hero's fate,
In tender strains, celestial Muse! relate.
The latent foe to friendship makes pretence,
The name assumes without the sacred sense!

22. This poem was first printed in the *Proceedings of the Massachusetts Historical Society,* VII (1863-64), 165-67, for October, 1863, with the following prefatory note: "The President [the Hon. Robert C. Winthrop] said that he had found among the Bowdoin Papers the original manuscript of a poem by the celebrated negro slave, Phillis Wheatley, on the capture of General Charles Lee by the British. It had never been printed, so far as he could ascertain. It was certainly not in either of the editions of the printed volumes of her poems. He then read it as follows:—." Phillis had intended to include it in her second book (see the "Proposal" reprinted in the appendix. Also see "A Rebus" in Part One, page 59, for information on Bowdoin). This and several other poems in this Part indicate Phillis' awareness of the military forces in the war. However, her poem is hardly in keeping with the facts. Her patriotism is proper, but she has Lee speak words near the end of the poem which are hardly in keeping with his great desire to replace Washington in command. Perhaps this is why Bowdoin never let the poem be published. However, Phillis was a civilian far from the place where Lee was captured, and she was therefore subject to many rumors. Charles Lee was taken prisoner on the night of December 13, 1776. Note that Phillis also used the term "Columbia" in this poem. (The Massachusetts Historical Society reports that it does not have the manuscript of this poem.)

He, with a rapture well dissembl'd, press'd
The hero's hand, and, fraudful, thus address'd,
"O friend belov'd! may heaven its aid afford,
And spread yon troops beneath thy conquering sword!
Grant to America's united prayer
A glorious conquest on the field of war!
But thou indulgent to my warm request,
Vouchsafe thy presence as my honour'd guest:
From martial cares a space unbend thy soul
In social banquet, and the sprightly bowl."
Thus spoke the foe; and warlike LEE reply'd,
"Ill fits it me, who such an army guide,
To whom his conduct each brave soldier owes,
To waste an hour in banquets or repose:
This day important, with loud voice demands
Our wisest Counsels, and our bravest hands."
Thus having said, he heav'd a boding sigh;
The hour approach'd that damps Columbia's Joy.
Inform'd, conducted by the treach'rous friend,
With winged speed the adverse train attend,
Ascend the Dome, and seize with frantic air
The self surrender'd glorious prize of war!
On sixty coursers, swifter than the wind,
They fly, and reach the British camp assign'd.
Arriv'd, what transport touch'd their leader's breast!
Who thus deriding, the brave Chief address'd.
"Say, art thou he, beneath whose vengeful hands
Our best of heroes grasp'd in death the sands?
One fierce regard of thine indignant eye
Turn'd Britain pale, and made her armies fly:
But Oh! how chang'd! a prisoner in our arms
Till martial honour, dreadful in her charms,
Shall grace Britannia at her sons' return,
And widow'd thousands in our triumphs mourn."
While thus he spoke, the hero of renown
Survey'd the boaster with a gloomy frown,
And stern reply'd: "Oh arrogrance of tongue!
And wild ambition, ever prone to wrong!

Believ'st thou chief, that armies such as thine
Can stretch in dust that heaven-defended line?
In vain allies may swarm from distant lands,
And demons aid in formidable bands.
Great as thou art, thou shun'st the field of fame,
Disgrace to Britain, and the British name!
When offer'd combat by the noble foe,
(Foe to mis-rule,) why did thy sword forego
The easy conquest of the rebel-land?
Perhaps *too* easy for thy martial hand.
What various causes to the field invite!
For plunder *you,* and we for freedom fight.
Her cause divine with generous ardor fires,
And every bosom glows as she inspires!
Already, thousands of your troops are fled
To the drear mansions of the silent dead:
Columbia too, beholds with streaming eyes
Her heroes fall—'tis freedom's sacrifice!
So wills the Power who with convulsive storms
Shakes impious realms, and nature's face deforms;
Yet those brave troops innum'rous as the sands
One soul inspires, one General Chief commands.
Find in your train of boasted heroes, one
To match the praise of Godlike Washington.
Thrice happy Chief! in whom the virtues join,
And heaven-taught prudence speaks the man divine!"
    He ceas'd. Amazement struck the warrior-train,
    And doubt of conquest, on the hostile plain.

BOSTON, Decr. 30, 1776.

Appendix

✤✤✤✤✤✤✤

Letters and Proposals for a Second Book

All but three of the extant letters by Phillis Wheatley were published in the *Proceedings of the Massachusetts Historical Society* for November, 1863 (Vol. VII, pp. 267-79). Therefore, all but those indicated otherwise are based on that printing. (Her letter to Washington has already been given with her poem to him, p. 87.) Of course, none of her extant letters would be of consequence without the fact of her poems. Unfortunately, only one of the thirteen letters which she proposed to put in her next book is still available.

Among the pertinent remarks given in introduction to the printing of her letters cited in the paragraph above are the following:

> [Mr. Deane told the Society that he had received the originals of the letters from the Rev. Edward E. Hale, "one of our associates, who kindly procured them for my use from Mrs. William Beecher, of Brookfield, to whom they belong. In a letter to Mr. Hale, dated October 23, 1863 . . . this lady writes:—"]
>
> They were given to me ages since by the person to whom they were addressed. She was then a very little, very old, very infirm, very, *very* black woman, with a great shock of the whitest of wool all over her head,—a picture well photographed on my mind's eye. She died in the odor of sanctity, sometime in 1833 or '4, an uncommonly pious, sensible, and intelligent woman, respected and visited by every person in Newport who could appreciate excellence.

Mr. Deane adds: "These letters, which are written in a beautiful hand, are addressed to a negro friend in Newport, R. I. (a young woman named Obour Tanner), probably serving in the same capacity as Phillis herself; and, from some expressions in the first letter, it may be inferred that they were both brought from Africa, and perhaps at the same time."

To Arbour Tanner, in Newport.

BOSTON May 19th 1772.

DEAR SISTER,—I rec'd your favour of February 6th for which I give you my sincere thanks. I greatly rejoice with you in that realizing view, and I hope experience, of the saving change which you so emphatically describe. Happy were it for us if we could arrive to that evangelical Repentance, and the true holiness of heart which you mention. Inexpressibly happy should we be could we have a due sense of the beauties and excellence of the crucified Saviour. In his Crucifixion may be seen marvellous displays of Grace and Love, sufficient to draw and invite us to the rich and endless treasures of his mercy; let us rejoice in and adore the wonders of God's infinite Love in bringing us from a land semblant of darkness itself, and where the divine light of revelation (being obscur'd) is as darkness. Here the knowledge of the true God and eternal life are made manifest; but there, profound ignorance overshadows the land. Your observation is true, namely, that there was nothing in us to recommend us to God. Many of our fellow creatures are pass'd by, when the bowels of divine love expanded toward us. May this goodness & long suffering of God lead us to unfeign'd repentance.

It gives me very great pleasure to hear of so many of my nation, seeking with eagerness the way of true felicity. O may we all meet at length in that happy mansion. I hope the correspondence between us will continue, (my being much indispos'd this winter past, was the reason of my not answering yours before now) which correspondence I hope may have the happy effect of improving our mutual friendship. Till we meet in the regions of consummate blessedness, let us endeavor by the assistance of divine grace, to live the life, and we shall die the death of the Righteous. May this be our happy case, and of those who are travelling to the region of Felicity, is the earnest request of your affectionate

Friend & humble servant PHILLIS WHEATLEY

To Arbour Tanner, in Newport. To the care of
Mr. Pease's Servant. Rhode Island.

BOSTON, July 19th, 1772.

MY DEAR FRIEND,—I rec'd your kind epistle a few days ago; much disappointed to hear that you had not rec'd my answer to your first letter. I have been in a very poor state of health all the past winter and spring, and now reside in the country for the benefit of its more wholesome air. I came to town this morning to spend the Sabbath with my master and mistress. Let me be interested in your prayers that God would please to bless to me the means us'd for my recovery, if agreeable to his holy will. While my outward man languishes under weakness and pa[in], may the inward be refresh'd and strengthen'd more abundantly by him who declar'd from heaven that his strength was made perfect in weakness! May he correct our vitiated taste, that the meditation of him may be delightful to us. No longer to be so excessively charm'd with fleeting vanities: but pressing forward to the fix'd mark for the prize. How happy that man who is prepar'd for that night wherein no man can work! Let us be mindful of our high calling, continually on our guard, lest our treacherous hearts should give the adversary an advantage over us. O! who can think without horror of the snares of the Devil. Let us, by frequent meditation on the eternal Judgment, prepare for it. May the Lord bless to us these thoughts, and teach us by his Spirit to live to him alone, and when we leave this world may we be his. That this may be our happy case, is the sincere desire

of, your affectionate friend, & humble serv't

PHILLIS WHEATLEY.

I sent the letter to Mr. Whitwell's who said he wou'd forward it.

To Obour Tanner, in New Port.

BOSTON Oct. 30, 1773.

DEAR OBOUR,—I rec'd your most kind epistles of Aug. 27th, & Oct. 13th, by a young man of your acquaintance, for which I am oblig'd to you. I hear of your welfare with pleasure; but this acquaints you that I am at present indispos'd by a cold, & since my arrival have been visited by the asthma.

Your observations on our dependence on the Deity, &

your hopes that my wants will be supply'd from his fulness which is in Christ Jesus, is truly worthy of your self. I can't say but my voyage to England has conduced to the recovery (in a great measure) of my health. The friends I found there among the nobility and gentry, their benevolent conduct towards me, the unexpected and unmerited civility and complaisance with which I was treated by all, fills me with astonishment. I can scarcely realize it. This I humbly hope has the happy effect of lessening me in my own esteem. Your reflections on the sufferings of the Son of God, & the inestimable price of our immortal souls, plainly demonstrate the sensations of a soul united to Jesus. What you observe of Esau is true of all mankind, who, (left to themselves) would sell their heavenly birth rights for a few moments of sensual pleasure, whose wages at last (dreadful wages!) is eternal condemnation. Dear Obour, let us not sell our birthright for a thousand worlds, which indeed would be as dust upon the balance. The God of the seas and dry land, has graciously brought me home in safety. Join with me in thanks to him for so great a mercy, & that it may excite me to praise him with cheerfulness, to persevere in Grace & Faith, & in the knowledge of our Creator and Redeemer,—that my heart may be fill'd with gratitude. I should have been pleas'd greatly to see Miss West, as I imagine she knew you. I have been very busy ever since my arrival, or should have now wrote a more particular account of my voyage, but must submit that satisfaction to some other opportunity. I am Dear friend,

Most affectionately ever yours.

PHILLIS WHEATLEY

My mistress has been very sick above 14 weeks, & confined to her bed the whole time, but is I hope somewhat better, now.

The young man by whom this is handed you seems to me to be a very clever man, knows you very well, & is very complaisant and agreeable. P. W.

I enclose Proposals for my book, and beg you'd use your interest to get subscriptions, as it is for my benefit.

To Miss Obour Tanner. Newport.[1]

BOSTON, March 21, 1774.

DEAR OBOUR,—I rec'd your obliging letter, enclos'd in your revd Pastor's & handed me by his son. I have lately met with a great trial in the death of my mistress; let us imagine the loss of a parent, sister, or brother, the tenderness of all these were united in her. I was a poor little outcast & a stranger when she took me in: not only into her house, but I presently became a sharer in her most tender affections. I was treated by her more like her child than her servant; no opportunity was left unimproved of giving me the best of advice; but in terms how tender! how engaging! This I hope ever to keep in remembrance. Her exemplary life was a greater monitor than all her precepts and instruction; thus we may observe of how much greater force example is than instruction. To alleviate our sorrows we had the satisfaction to see her depart in inexpressible raptures, earnest longings, & impatient thirstings for the *upper* courts of the Lord. Do, my dear friend, remember me & this family in your closet, that this afflicting dispensation may be sanctify'd to us. I am very sorry to hear that you are indispos'd, but hope this will find you in better health. I have been unwell the greater part of the winter, but am much better as the spring approaches. Pray excuse my not writing to you so long before, for I have been so busy lately that I could not find leisure. I shall send the 5 books you wrote for, the first convenient opportunity; if you want more, they shall be ready for you. I am very affectionately your friend,

PHILLIS WHEATLEY

To Miss Obour Tanner, New Port, Rhode Island.
favd by Mr. Pemberton.

DEAR OBOUR,—I rec'd last evening your kind & friendly letter and am not a little animated thereby. I hope ever to follow your good advices and be resigned to the afflicting hand of a seemingly frowning Providence. I have rec'd the

1. A "heliotype *fac-simile*" of this letter may be seen in the *Proceedings of the Massachusetts Historical Society,* XV (1876-77), between pp. 386 and 387, in the number for December, 1877.

money you sent for the 5 books & 2/6 more for another, which I now send & wish safe to hand. Your tenderness for my welfare demands my gratitude Assist me, dear Obour! to praise our great benefactor, for the innumerable benefits continually pour'd upon me, that while he strikes one comfort *dead* he raises up another. But O that I could dwell on & delight in him alone above every other object! While the world hangs loose about us we shall not be in painful *anxiety* in giving up to God that which he first gave to us. Your letter came by Mr. Pemberton who brings you the book you write for. I shall wait upon Mr. Whitwell with your letter and am

Dear sister, ever affectionately, your

PHILLIS WHEATLEY

I have rec'd by some of the last ships 300 more of my Poems. BOSTON May 6, 1774.

Miss Obour Tanner, Worcester.

BOSTON May 29th '78.

DEAR OBOUR,—I am exceedingly glad to hear from you by Mrs. Tanner, and wish you had timely notice of her departure, so as to have wrote me; next to that is the pleasure of hearing that you are well. The vast variety of scenes that have pass'd before us these 3 years past, will to a reasonable mind serve to convince us of the uncertain duration of all things temporal, and the proper result of such a consideration is an ardent desire of, & preparation for, a state and enjoyments which are more suitable to the immortal mind. You will do me a great favour if you'll write me by every opportunity. Direct your letters under cover to Mr. John Peters in Queen Street. I have but half an hour's notice; and must apologize for this hasty scrawl. I am most affectionately, My dear Obour, your sincere friend

PHILLIS WHEATLEY.

Miss Obour Tanner, Worcester. favd by Cumberland.

BOSTON May 10, 1779.

DR. OBOUR,—By this opportunity I have the pleasure to inform you that I am well and hope you are so; tho' I have been silent, I have not been unmindful of you, but a variety of hindrances was the cause of my not writing to you. But in time to come I hope our correspondence will revive—and revive in better times—pray write me soon, for I long to hear from you—you may depend on constant replies —I wish you much happiness, and am

Dr. Obour, your friend & sister

PHILLIS PETERS.

To the Rev. Mr. Samuel Hopkins, of New Port, Rhode Island.[2]

BOSTON, Feb. 9, 1774.

Rev'd Sir,—I take with pleasure the opportunity by the Post, to acquaint you with the arrival of my books from London. I have sealed up a package containing 17 for you, and 2 for Mr. Tanner, and one for Mrs. Mason, and only wait for you to appoint some proper person, by whom I may convey them to you. I received some time ago 20*s* sterling upon them, by the hands of your son, in a letter from Abour Tanner. I received at the same time a paper, by which I understand there are two negro men, who are desirous of returning to their native country, to preach the Gospel; but being much indisposed by the return of my asthmatic complaint, besides the sickness of my mistress, who has been long confined to her bed, and is not expected to live a great while; all these things render it impracticable for me to do anything at present with regard to that paper, but what I can do in influencing my Christian friends and acquaint-

2. In *The Journal of Negro History,* XXXIV (1949), 462-64, Benjamin Quarles points out that there is a letter from Phillis Wheatley embedded in a letter from Joshua Coffin to John Greenleaf Whittier dated April 29, 1839, which Whittier published in the *Pennsylvania Freeman* for May 9, 1839. The beginning of Coffin's letter and the embedded letter from Phillis Wheatley are reprinted there. Coffin says that he found the letter in Phillis' handwriting in the "rich and valuable collection of pamphlets, manuscripts, and autographs, in the possession of the Rev. W. B. Sprague, D. D." of Albany. Coffin continues, "It is beautifully written, and with the consent of the good Doctor, I herewith send you a copy, verbatim et literatim, from the original." Her letter is to the Rev. Samuel Hopkins, pastor of the First Congregational Church in Newport. The reprinting here is based on that in *The Journal of Negro History.*

ances, to promote this laudable design, shall not be wanting. Methinks, Rev. Sir, this is the beginning of that happy period foretold by the Prophets, when all shall know the Lord from the least to the greatest, and that without the assistance of human Art or Eloquence. My heart expands with sympathetic joy to see at distant time the thick cloud of ignorance dispersing from the face of my benighted country. Europe and America have long been fed with the heavenly provision, and I fear they loath it, while Africa is perishing with a spiritual Famine. O that they could partake of the crumbs, the precious crumbs, which fall from the table of these distinguished children of the kingdom.

Their minds are unprejudiced against the truth, therefore 'tis to be hoped they would receive it with their whole heart. I hope that which the divine royal Psalmist says by inspiration is now on the point of being accomplished, namely, Ethiopia shall soon stretch forth her hands unto God. Of this, Abour Tanner, and I trust many others within your knowledge, are living witnesses. Please to give my love to her, and I intend to write her soon. My best respects attend every kind inquiry after your obliged Humble servant,

PHILLIS WHEATLEY

To the Earl of Dartmouth[3]

My Lord

The Joyful occacion which has given me this Confidence in Addressing your Lordship in the inclosed peice will, I hope sufficiently apologize for this freedom in an African who with the now happy America exults with equal trans-

3. Although this letter is cited in Vernon Loggins, *The Negro Author* (New York, 1931), to the best of my knowledge this is the first time that it has been printed. The above is based on a photocopy of a manuscript kindly supplied by the Massachusetts Historical Society, which has the original. The enclosure she refers to was the poem to Dartmouth later printed in the 1773 volume and reprinted in Part One, page 33. The manuscript in the possession of the Massachusetts Historical Society may be a first draft or a copy, judging from the carelessness of handwriting, spelling, and punctuation, as contrasted with the other Phillis Wheatley manuscripts of poems and letters which are extant. Indeed, the handwriting may not even be hers, though the letter certainly is. Note her intention to include this letter in the proposed second volume which is outlined following this letter.

port in the view of one of its greatest advocates presiding with the Special tenderness of a Fatherly Heart over that Department.

Nor can they my Lord be insensible of the Friendship so much exemplified in your Endeavours in their behalf during the late unhappy Disturbances

I sincerely wish your Lordship all possible success in your Undertaking for the Interest of north America

That the united blessings of Heaven & Earth may attend you here and the endless Felicity of the invisible State in the presence of the divine ["divine" is inserted above the line and indicated with a caret] Benefactor may be your portion hereafter is the hearty Desire of

My Lord
Your Lordships
Most Obedient
H'ble Servant

Boston N. E. Octo. 10th 1772 Phillis Wheatley

✤✤✤✤✤✤✤

PROPOSALS,[4]

For printing by subscription a volume of Poems & Letters on various subjects, dedicated to the Right Hon. Benjamin Franklin Esq: One of the Ambassadors of the United States at the Court of France,

4. This was first printed in the *Evening Post and General Advertiser* of October 30, 1779, occupying a full column on the front page. It was reprinted in the same paper on November 6 and 27, and December 4, 11, and 18. White and Adams were also printers of the *Post*. The proposed volume was never published. Of the items listed, only the poems on General Lee, to General Washington, and the two to Lieutenant R——— of the Royal Navy, and the letter to Dartmouth are extant—all included in this volume. Unfortunately, Phillis' husband disappeared with her papers, and we do not know what happened to them. However, judging from our experiences with the Lee and Washington poems and the Dartmouth letter, copies or originals of some others of these items may yet turn up. This reprinting of the "Proposals" is based on that in the *Proceedings of the Massachusetts Historical Society* in the September, 1865, number (VIII [1864-65], 461-62). (For a note on Admiral Montague, see her poem to the gentleman of the Navy in Part Two, page 82.) A second volume was proposed again in 1784 (see Part Two, note 21).

Poems.

Thoughts on the Times.

On the Capture of General Lee, to I. B. Esq.

To his Excellency General Washington.

On the death of General Wooster.

An Address to Dr —— ——.

To Lieut R—— of the Royal Navy.

To the same.

To T. M. Esq. of Granada.

To Sophia of South Carolina.

To Mr. A. M'B—— of the Navy.

To Lieut R—— D—— of the Navy.

Ocean.

The choice and advantages of a Friend; to Mr. T—— M——.

Farewell to England 1773.

To Mrs. W—ms on Anna Eliza.

To Mr. A. McB—d.

Epithalamium to Mrs. H—— ——.

To P. N. S. & Lady on the death of their infant son.

To Mr. El—y on the death of his Lady.

On the death of Lieut. L—ds.

To Penelope.

To Mr. & Mrs. L—— on the death of their daughter.

A Complaint.

To Mr. A. I. M. on Virtue.

To Dr. L—d and Lady on the death of their son aged 5 years.

To Mr. L—g on the death of his son.

To Capt. F—r on the death of his granddaughter.

To Philandra an Elegy.

Niagara.

Chloe to Calliope.

To Musidora on Florello.

To Sir E. L—— Esq.

To the Hon. John Montague Esq. Rear Admiral of the Blue.

Letters.

1 To the Right Hon. Wm E. of Dartmouth, Sec. of State of N. America.

2 To the Rev. Mr. T. P. Framington.

3 To Mr. T. W.—Dartmouth College.

4 To the Hon. T. H. Esq.

5 To Dr. B. Rush, Phila.

6 To the Rev. Dr. Thomas, London.

7 To the Right Hon. Countess of H——.

8 To I. M—— Esq. London.

9 To Mrs. W—e in the County of Surrey.

10 To Mr. T. M. Homerton, near London.

11 To Mrs. S. W——.

12 To the Rt. Hon. the Countess of H——.

13 To the same.

MESSIEURS PRINTERS,—The above collection of Poems and Letters was put into my hands by the desire of the ingenious author, in order to be introduced to public View.

The subjects are various and curious, and the author a *female African,* whose lot it was to fall into the hands of a *generous* master and *great* benefactor.

The learned and ingenuous, as well as those who are pleased with novelty, are invited to incourage the publication by a generous subscription—the former that they may fan the sacred fire which is self-enkindled in the breast of this *young* African—The ingenuous that they may by reading this collection have a large play for their imaginations, and be excited to please and benefit mankind by some brilliant production of their own pens.—Those who are *always* in search of some new thing, that they may obtain a sight of this *rara avis in terra*—And every one that the ingenious author may be encouraged to improve her own mind, benefit and please mankind.

CONDITIONS.

They will be printed on good paper and a neat Type; and will contain about 300 Pages in Octavo.

The price to Subscribers will be *Twelve Pounds,* neatly Bound & Lettered, and *Nine Pounds* sew'd in blue paper, one Half to be paid on Subscribing, the other Half on delivery of the Books.

The Work will be put to the Press as soon as a sufficient Number of Encouragers offer.

Those who subscribe for Six Books will have a Seventh Gratis.

Subscriptions are taken by White and Adams, the Publishers, in School-Street, Boston.

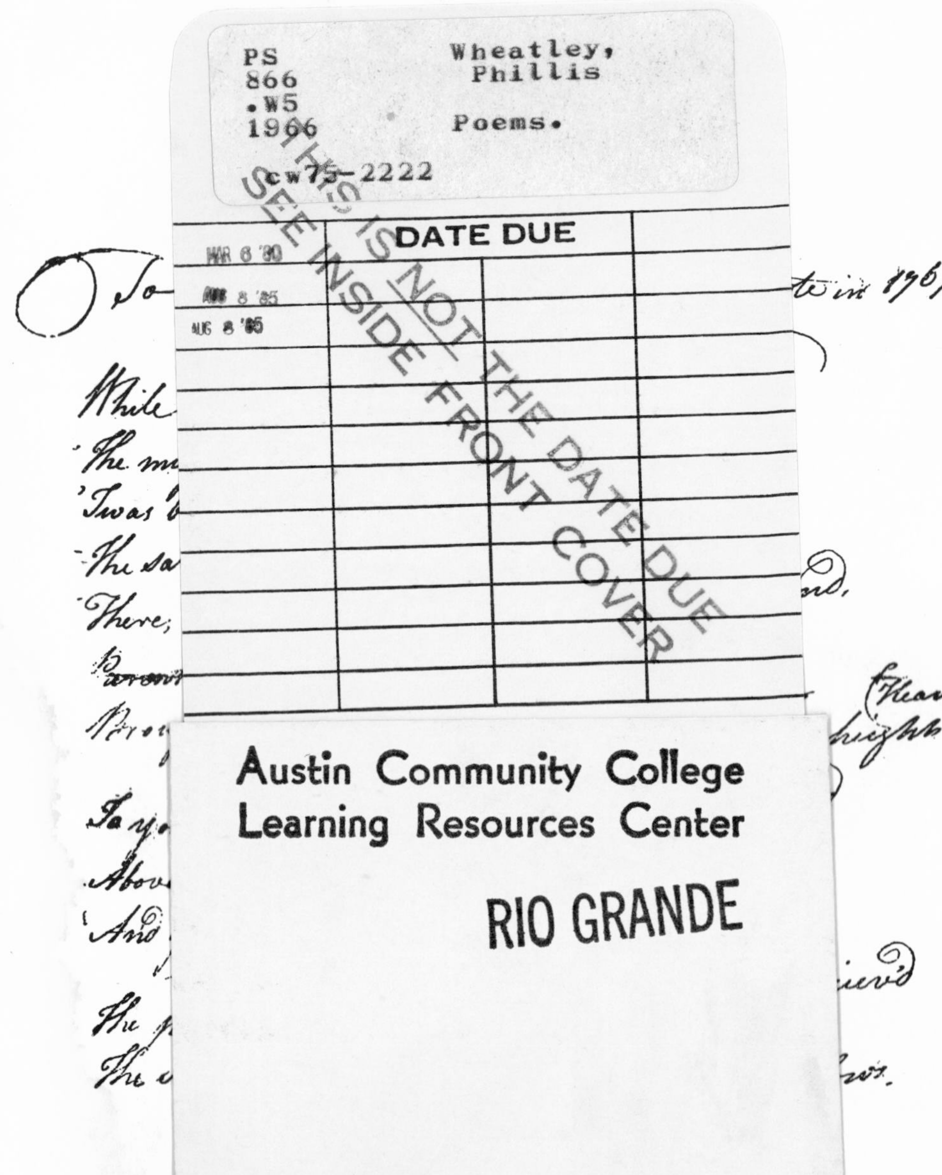
PS
866
.W5
1966
Wheatley,
Phillis
Poems.
cw75-2222
THIS IS NOT THE DATE DUE
SEE INSIDE FRONT COVER
DATE DUE
MAR 6 '80
AUG 8 '85
AUG 8 '85
Austin Community College
Learning Resources Center
RIO GRANDE